I0661013

Alexander K. Mcclure

The South

its industrial, financial, and political condition

Alexander K. McClure

The South
its industrial, financial, and political condition

ISBN/EAN: 9783337078775

Printed in Europe, USA, Canada, Australia, Japan

Cover: Foto ©Suzi / pixelio.de

More available books at **www.hansebooks.com**

THE SOUTH:

ITS

INDUSTRIAL, FINANCIAL,

AND

POLITICAL CONDITION.

BY

A. K. McCLURE.

PHILADELPHIA:
J. B. LIPPINCOTT COMPANY.
1886.

Copyright, 1886, by A. K. McClure.

CONTENTS.

INTRODUCTION.

THIS work is presented without any pretence of literary merit. It gives, in carefully-revised chapters, the results of several recent journeys in the Southern States, during which the grave political, business, and race problems were dispassionately and industriously studied; and the fact that a few of the chapters, written as long as five years ago, are more than vindicated by the rapid progress of the South in all that makes material advancement, fully warrants the later and more hopeful view of early Southern prosperity.

Believing that we are soon to date the turn of the tide of foreign immigration from the West to the South; that we are soon to note a rapid migration of skilled labor from the North to the South; that

Northern capital will, at an early day, turn Southward to manufacture iron, mine and ship coal, spin
and weave cotton, and rear machine-shops; and that
the surplus population of our fields, our mines, our
forests, and our mills will gradually but surely seek
the better facilities for requited industry in the Southern States, I offer the suggestions of these pages for
the considerate judgment of progressive people of
both sections.

There are yet lingering sectional prejudices in both
North and South, and they have greatly hindered the
rehabilitation of the impoverished insurgent States;
but the war now belongs to the memories of more
than twenty years ago; its warriors of blue and gray
are rapidly passing to join the great majority that
has gone before, and a new generation is fast filling
the places of the men of the generation that fought
the most heroic battles of history. The victories of
peace are now to become their chaplets, and the surplus capital and industry of the North will soon be
inseparably interwoven with the New South. To
hasten the complete restoration of fraternal and busi-

ness intercourse between the North and South, and thereby enlarge the prosperity of both, is the aim of these chapters, and if they shall, even in a feeble way, contribute to that grand consummation, the author will be more than compensated for his labor.

A. K. M.

PHILADELPHIA, May, 1886.

THE SOUTH:

ITS INDUSTRIAL, FINANCIAL, AND POLITICAL CONDITION.

ARLINGTON, THE HOME OF LEE.

ONE of the mellowest of early winter days tempted me to revisit the historic Arlington Mansion, once the palatial and hospitable home of Robert E. Lee. It is visible from almost any point in Washington, although several miles distant on the sunny side of the Potomac. Its massive white Grecian columns, half hidden by the native forest on the north and south, are unobscured by the evergreens and few monarchs of the primeval Virginia wilderness which survive on the gentle, undulating slopes from the heights down to the silver line that divides Washington from the Mother of Presidents. The beautiful Capitol and the Arlington Mansion face each other, and present the most attractive views from their respective eminences. Looking from the western windows of the Capitol, across to the crescent of hills that skirts the Virginia side of the Potomac, Arlington first attracts the eyes of the observer, and the distance of several miles is none too great to lend the grandest enchantment to what was the proudest of Southern homes but twenty-five years ago. The ravages of the gnawing tooth of time; the widened seams between the once faultless lines of masonry; the blistered and scaling colors which deform the surface of pillar, wall, and door; the countless marks of decay which tell the story of the deserted home and the stay of the stranger,—all these are effaced from the picture by the distant gaze, and Arlington looks as beautiful and as homelike as it was when Lee made his last sad journey across the river as an officer of the army that pointed to him as one of its brightest ornaments. Like Scott, on whose staff he was the most beloved and trusted, Lee was a Virginian, and his resignation was one of the keenest blows that had then been felt by his chief. Both were sorrow-stricken at the separation to draw their swords upon each other; and there is little doubt that Lee would have halted at the threshold, could he have foreseen that his devotion to his mother Common-wealth would make him the captain in a struggle for a new nationality that must have perished more ingloriously had it won its battles, than was its recall to the Union by the sword.

I had visited Arlington but once before, and the day was a memorable one. Charleston, the city that had long been cherishing rebellion, had just been captured after many disastrous failures to possess that Confederate stronghold. While standing on the broad, unevenly-tiled portico of Arlington, looking out between the great columns to the Capital that seemed then for the first time in four years to be safe from the insurgent, the hour of noon was struck by the signal-gun of Fort Whipple, hard by, and as quick as sound could fly to report the command, a thousand guns responded from hill to hill, shouting their hoarse song of victory over the Lost Cause. What appeared to the casual observer as simply a cluster of wooded ridges along the Virginia shore, belched forth their columns of smoke and thundered to the world the tidings that free government had not

perished from the earth. Full half a generation has
passed since then, and change has wrought sub-
lime achievements in all sections of the country
during twenty years of peace; but Arlington is only
twenty years older, as is told by the ceaseless offices
of decay, and there the story ends. Its history has
not abated in public interest. It is still the one
home, next to Mount Vernon, around which cluster
the fondest memories of Washington, and the sad
retribution that followed the estrangement of Lee
from his country is known in every section and
clime. His memory is cherished in Virginia and
in the South in a wealth of affection, and as the
clouds of passion are clearing away in the North,
there is naught but respect and sorrow for the Chris-
tian soldier who so loved a State as to be misguided
to fraternal war that widened into boundless bereavement and desolation.

A heartsome drive through Washington, with its
broad and well-paved streets, its varied architecture
in its cheerful-looking homes, its innumerable parks
and tri-angled greens, and its many monuments of
the country's greatness, brings you to Georgetown,
where Washington aristocracy reigns unsullied by
mixture with the promoted plebeian or the adventurer

of the Capital. Thence a rickety bridge, dilapidated in everything but the measure of its tolls, lands the visitor on the sacred soil of the once proud Old Dominion. There are few evidences remaining of the fortifications which displayed bristling guns when last I journeyed to Arlington. The ruder of the structures hastily erected to serve the purposes of war are seen here and there, with decay stamped upon them, and fenceless fields tell how the indolence and thriftlessness of slavery yet rule. Not until the well-beaten road turns into the pillared gate that opens the National Cemetery are there signs of care and industry; but the long, regular, white lines which traverse the carefully-garnished lawns tell a strange and sad story of war's multiplied retributions. Throughout the winding roads which gradually ascend the heights to the Arlington Mansion the grave-stone is never out of sight; and around the gardens up to the very pillars of the home of Lee the dreamless couches of Union officers are spread as if their dust was to stand as a line of eternal sentries about the tenantless halls of the Confederate chieftain. Twelve thousand warriors people this beautiful City of the Silent, and the Blue and the Gray sleep their long sleep together,—heroic

2*

enemies in the flame of battle, they have gained the peace that is to be unbroken. One-third of the whole number are the nameless tombs of the unknown, but their rest is undisturbed by the pity of the stranger, or the sorrowing of loved ones who mourn their unshrined dead. In one central vault the long-unearthed and scattered bones of over two thousand fallen soldiers have been gathered for sepulchre. Who they were when they braved the deadly strife; whether they were friend or foe, none can tell.

When the ravages of war had ceased, the government was but just to all in gleaning the battle-fields, where heroism such as was never surpassed in ancient or modern conflicts had been displayed by North and South, and rescuing the remains of all from desecration. In the centre of one of the broad lawns which are dotted with the white records of the sacrifices of war, on a little eminence that greets the early rays of the morning sun, is an enclosure in which there are monuments differing from the plain and uniform slabs noting the sleepers beneath them. It is neatly paled, carefully preserved, and looks as if the offices of affection had been freely exercised in guarding the ashes that repose there. It is the family burial-ground of the Custises and the Lees, and it is made the special care of those who are charged with the keeping of this vast tenement of the silent. Here and there may be seen wooden slabs of uniform size, conspicuous because higher than the modest marble that shapes its faultless lines on the levelled green. They are the graves of the Confederates who were left on the sanguinary field or who died within the Union lines, and they rest surrounded by those who were their deadly foes in battle. Over two hundred acres are enclosed in the cemetery, embracing Arlington Mansion in the centre and the now terraced and beautiful lawn that made the prospect so pleasing from the portico, when looking to the distant Capital, or to the calm blue waters of the Potomac. The entrance to the walled enclosure is fitly ornamented by pillars from the old War and Navy Buildings, and weather-beaten guns and symmetrically-rounded mounds of shot mark the many hillocks which so grandly variegate the slopes of Arlington Heights. Close to the mansion is the rude and yet attractive open temple, where Decoration Day is celebrated. The rostrum is flanked by the old Grecian pillars from the dismantled Departments of War in Washington, and the ivy, the jessamine, and the wild flower mingle their tributes to the martyrs of Freedom with the once terrible but now decorative engines of war. Just outside the wall is Fort Whipple, the central figure of the great family of defensive works that once rested on these hills. Its embankments are levelled, its ditches filled up, and its cannon deposed, and where the soldier watched his shotted gun is a large, level centre square, with many neat buildings about it. It is now the school of instruction for the signal and storm corps, and the epauletted and sworded gentry are training men to master the elements instead of teaching them the art of destruction. All around it on the many commanding eminences may yet be seen the crumbling earthworks of the almost unbroken chain of fortifications that more than half surrounded Washington; but they are ungarrisoned now, and the drum-beat no longer breaks the morning silence on the Virginia side of the Potomac.

The Arlington Mansion and its surrounding buildings have suffered no changes since Lee went to Richmond in 1861, never to return to his home, save such as the ceaseless work of decay has wrought. The doors and windows have faded; the pillars have decayed and scaled into ugliness; the narrow, ill-balustraded stairway is worn and battered; the empty rooms seem to give out more repulsive echoes of loneliness; the hearths are crumbling with weariness of vacancy, and it looks as if the hoot of the owl and the flap of the bat should break the painful solitude that reigns where George Washington Parke Custis and Robert E. Lee made one of the most brilliant and hospitable homes of Virginia. The soldier in blue, with an armless sleeve, has kept faithful vigil over this vast sepulchre for many years. He keeps the graves green, the flowers in bloom, the evergreens in shapely beauty, and all is neatness about the venerable mansion that is now the central citadel of the voiceless thousands around it; but the storms of nearly fourscore winters have beaten against Arlington and their ravages have been left to tell their own story. But of what moment is this desolation of all the attributes of home? Arlington is now only the mansion of the dead. Turn to every portico and window, and naught but the marks of the grave appear in contrast with the forest and its green sod; and at stated distances around the walks to the very columns of the mansion are the tombs of officers, standing like mute but inexorable sentinels to make the Lees strangers to the home they so much reverenced. The vengeful hand of Stanton has left its imprint everywhere about Arlington in the ghastly army it has summoned to forbid the Confederate chieftain's return, and its work is irrevocable. Since then the conquered insurgent warrior and the implacable War Minister have passed away. Off in the Virginia mountains, where the soldier of Arlington spent the evening of his life in usefulness, his dust rests within his college walls, and the repose that life refused to Stanton has been found in the grave. The beloved mistress of Arlington quickly followed her honored liege to that bourne whence no traveller returns, and the sons of Lee, who bravely but unobtrusively followed his fortunes in war, now fill his chair at Washington and Lee University and till the soil of the peninsula, while his trooper kinsman, Fitz-Hugh Lee, is Governor of the mother Commonwealth. The great actors who have written the strange records of Arlington have gone to their final account, and with the Judge of all the living they have their reward.

RICHMOND—VIRGINIA.

THE world moves, as Senator Brown recently advised the Georgia Legislature, and it moves in the South as well as elsewhere. It moves more slowly amidst the desolation the war left as the heritage of the South, as capital, labor, and enterprise had to be created or learned anew, but when the iron-horse sweeps over the Long Bridge at the rate of a mile a minute, and hurries down the Potomac and across the Virginia plains to Richmond in three and a half hours from Washington, there is progress in the South. For years after the war it was a tedious day's journey from the national to the Virginia capital, but now it is merely a pleasant excursion from one city to the other and back between breakfast and dinner. And Virginia is moving, sluggishly it is true, but moving nevertheless and in the right direction. Her homes are more heartsome and thrifty in their outward looks;

her fields give the assurance of greater plenty, and the gradual revival of hopeful energy will eventually obliterate the blight of the bondman and the terrible throes of his deliverance. Fredericksburg looks brighter than I have seen it at any time during the last fifteen years, and but for the dotted hill hard by, recalling the widespread bereavement that came to North and South when Burnside and Lee belched forth their deadly thunders at each other, there would be nothing about the ancient village to denote the shock of the battle that made it almost one vast charnel-house. The flag that waves high over the mingled dust of the blue and the gray, tells the stranger of victor and vanquished; but the fierce enemies who frowned upon each other behind their respective works, and the warriors themselves who met in the most sanguinary strife, are now so intermingled in the social and business circles of to-day that the war is remembered only as a horrible dream.

As you approach Richmond the evidences of improvement multiply, and there are few monuments to testify to the fearful struggle of four years that had the possession of this city for its objective-point. There is nothing to remind the traveller that more than two hundred thousand men fell in the struggle for Richmond. The signs of peace only are visible in the apparently comfortable community that surrounds the city and in the busy marts of trade exhibited in the narrow and sinuous streets which climb its broken hills. One pyramid monument of unhewn and mortarless stone, on an eminence in the northern suburb, is the general tribute of the survivors of the Lost Cause to their dead, and the statue of Jackson, a gift from sympathizing English- ∨ men, tells the whole story of Confederate heroism that is given in the poetry of the sculptor's chisel. Libby Prison has changed owners at the auction-block, and is now laden with the fruits of peaceful industry instead of housing a mass of sick and starving prisoners; and Belle Isle no longer answers the babblings of the waters of the James with the hoarse murmurs of despairing men. The plough-share has levelled the net-work of battlements which environed the dual capital, and the rustling corn and the waving wheat gladden the heart where the sentinel pursued his steady beat and the shotted guns awaited the signal of death. The venerable State-House that stands on the pinnacle of the city, surrounded by beautiful shades and exquisite monuments of the fathers of the Republic, has

3

braved the storms of nearly a century. It was
modelled by Jefferson after a Roman temple that
pleased his curious eye when abroad, and it was
erected before Washington was President, and when
the eloquence of Henry was heard in the House
of Delegates. It is rusted from foundation to
dome, and every feature of it tells the story of
neglected age; but what a history is interwoven
with its blistered pillars and seamed walls! Founded
by those most illustrious in the annals of free
government; the oldest capital of the Union; the
centre of the omnipotent power of the Old Dominion for a full generation; the cradle in which
the boasted Mother of Presidents reared her family
of rulers; the temple of Confederate authority for
four long years of sacrifice and waste; next the
forum where the enfranchised slave made laws for
his discomfited master, and then the triumphant
repudiator ran riot in its halls and scourged the
dismembered Commonwealth with shame.

The great stain on the Virginia of to-day is the repudiation frenzy that possessed her poverty-stricken
people under the inspiration of cunning ambition.
Unlike the other States which cast their fortunes
with the Confederacy, Virginia has had no debt cast

upon her by the thieving adventurer. The carpet-
bagger has never vexed her people by climbing into
her places of high authority. Since reconstruction
her government has been uniformly the creation of
her own citizens, and her Executives have maintained
the traditional integrity of old-time Virginia Governors. Her debt was all contracted before the war,
and is in no degree the invention of the stranger.
In the days of Virginia power and pride she built
great arteries of trade by land and water, and but for
the gnawing tooth of servile labor, she would have
more than rivalled Pennsylvania in material progress
and wealth, as she did in the mastery of her statesmanship. But in an evil day the Confederacy
reached out its arms, gathered the Old Dominion in
its fatal embrace, and thus dated her decline and fall.
Her territory was parted, and West Virginia was
greeted as the deformed birth of civil war. The
State became one vast battle-field, and the horrors of
bloody fraternal strife were concentrated upon the
people. Her lands were laid waste, her slave labor
welcomed to freedom, her wealth destroyed, and the
shadow of the avenging angel fell upon every house-
hold. And when peace came her immediate resources were wellnigh destroyed, poverty was the

rule even where fortune and plenty had smiled, and debt had been sleepless in its accumulation. The rich mines and forests and natural highways of West Virginia had been taken from her, and her nearly fifty millions of debt and suspended interest confronted her. To her credit let it be said that even in those days of sorest trial for Virginians, none heard the voice of the repudiationist. Her first administration chosen by the vote of her people of both races equitably divided the common debt of the two Virginias by funding the principal and accumulated interest of two-thirds of the whole amount as the debt of Virginia, and issuing certificates for the remaining third as a claim against West Virginia. The interest coupons were made receivable for taxes, and all felt a just pride in the vindication of Virginia credit under what is known as the Walker Funding Bill. But taxes were heavy because there was little wherewith to pay them, and the apparent liquidation of one-third of the debt by an order on West Virginia opened the way for a repudiation movement that has finally triumphed over all the traditions and pride of Virginia integrity. Disappointed ambition seized upon the easy way to pay debts by repudiating them, and carried the issue to the hustings, where the exactions of poverty made men hesitate between duty and dishonor. The funding act was defeated by legislative embarrassments, although repudiation was disclaimed by all. Then came Mr. Hugh Mc-Culloch, who proposed to fund the whole debt of about thirty-two millions in forty-year bonds, to bear three per cent. for ten years, four per cent. for fifteen years, and five per cent. thereafter, and the coupons to be receivable for taxes.

The bill was passed and the eight millions required by the act were funded within the time prescribed; but General Mahone then entered the field as a full-fledged repudiationist, divided the white Democrats by appeals to ambition and faction, flattered the colored voters into his ranks by lavish promises of a free ballot without any taxes whatever, commanded the aid of the few white Republican leaders by open barter of office and political success, and the McCulloch funding scheme was arrested by the growth of repudiation and the peril of trusting the solemn faith of the once proud Old Dominion. By the consolidation of the colored vote and the aid of the Republican leaders as a political expedient, Mahone carried the Legislature, elected himself to the United States Senate, deposed

3*

every debt-paying State official within the reach of
the legislative power, chose repudiation County
Judges in most of the districts of the State, passed
an act distinctly repudiating all of the debt over
twenty millions, and carried an amendment to the
Constitution removing all tax qualifications for elec-
tors. Riddleberger, the author of the repudiation
measure in the Legislature, logically followed Mahone to the United States Senate; but the arts of
the demagogue win only perishable triumphs, and
Virginia has re-asserted herself by the election of
Lee as Chief Magistrate, and her repudiation Senators
will soon seek the shades of grateful oblivion. The
stain of repudiation cannot be effaced; its work
cannot be undone, but the tide of public dishonesty
has been arrested in its steady march toward universal repudiation, and the venerable Commonwealth
will build anew on the racked foundations of State
pride and honor. The special message of Governor
Lee sent to the Legislature in February last, tells
the whole story. The Riddleberger settlement of
the debt will not be disturbed, for the simple reason
that any administration or any party attempting to
renew the agitation, would be hopelessly overthrown. It was that obvious truth that compelled

Governor Lee, who earnestly opposed every form of repudiation, to say in his message that "if the creditors could be fully informed of the true state of affairs, they would accept the provisions of the Riddleberger bill." But for the defeat of the open Repudiationists at the late election, there is little reason to doubt that the hesitation of the creditors to accept the Riddleberger basis, and the recent decisions of the Supreme Court of the United States, would have been made the pretext for another and more sweeping plunge into dishonor.

It is due to the people of Virginia to say that it was not the property-owners and tax-payers, as a rule, who were repudiators. A fraction of the Democrats separated from the regular organization under the leadership of Mahone. The readjustment of the debt was only their nominal aim, while the control of the State, the partition of its offices, and the punishment of the so-called Bourbons were the real purposes in view. They allied the whole colored vote with them by cunningly devised appeals to their cupidity and ambition. The negroes, as a rule, do not pay taxes on property, but they were taxed with all non-property-holding whites one dollar per capita as a prerequisite for voting, and the capitation tax went to the free school fund that is devoted to the equal education of whites and blacks. The repudiationists appealed to the colored voters by proposing to abolish the capitation tax, and thus enable all to vote without the payment of taxes at all. Thus the eighty thousand colored voters were practically secured for repudiation, although they were repudiating their own free schools by their own act; and thus, mainly by the vote of non-taxpayers and adventurers in politics, the debt of Virginia was repudiated against the protest of a large majority of the actual tax-payers of the State. Those who must pay whatever debt shall be paid are not the repudiationists, but numbers and corrupt combinations will often defeat property and honesty.

THE SISTER CAROLINAS.

THE New South! We have heard that expression many times during the last twenty years, but it never had the meaning that it has to-day. We had a New South when the war closed,—a South with slavery violently abolished, and with poverty, desolation, and wide-spread despair the heritage of her people, and a South unschooled in progress, save as the severe necessities of war had impressed their lessons. We talked of the New South again when reconstruction had completed its work in the tempest of partisan and sectional passion, but it was the greater sweep of desolation of peace that followed the desolation of war. Then came the New South, when intelligence, integrity, and property gained the mastery in local government. It was achieved only after many years of bewildering debauchery and waste in authority, and of wanton humiliation to all who refused homage to ignorance and theft; but it came with the first

29

bright silver lining to the dark clouds of war and reconstruction, and it dated the beginning of the deliverance of the South from the fearfully retributive fruits of civil war. The South is often censured for its ready submission to the memorable electoral crime of 1876; but had all the interests of home, of property, of peace and self-respect appealed to the North as they appealed to the South, when the State governments of South Carolina, Florida, and Louisiana trembled in the balance of fraud, there would have been quite as prompt submission to a fraudulent presidential title north of the Potomac as there was south of its historic banks. And when it is remembered that to have refused submission would have been stamped as a supplementary rebellion against authority under color of law, and against the army with Grant at its head, there was sound discretion in the submissive South. That monstrous electoral fraud fixed its own infamy indelibly in the annals of the nation, by recognizing the Democratic Governors elected on the same ticket with Tilden in the three States that were despoiled of their electoral votes, and there is a measure of historic justice in the re-election of Vice-President Hendricks that would have been rounded out in the grandest completeness, had not

the infirmities of time dimmed the lustre of achievements in the life of Samuel J. Tilden. The New
South of to-day would have dated eight years earlier
had not the decisive judgment of the nation been
overthrown in crime, but there is now vastly riper
fitness for improving all the logical advantages of the
disenthralment of the South than there could have
been in 1877.

There are few, even among the more intelligent
people of the North, who can justly appreciate the
New South of to-day. Only those who have freely
mingled with the Southern people during the last
fifteen years, and carefully noted their condition and
the restraints and obstacles which confronted them in
every effort at manly progress, can understand the
full meaning of the words, the New South, as they
are understood to-day. They have a practical meaning that only the South can understand, and yet they
inspire no single hope or wish to undo that which
has been done. The Southern eye brightens, and the
Southern face beams with hope, as the future of the
South is discussed, but there is no turning with wist-
ful eyes to the theories of the past. The Old South
is dead. It has passed away; it is buried; it is forgotten, save as old memories and old pride cast their

flitting shadows over the better present and brighter future. I have heard no Southern man talk of the past as a guide for the future. A new generation has come from the cradle to manhood since Sumter was fired upon, and they, with the surviving Southern soldiery, understand the irrevocable arbitrament of the sword. And they understand, also, that it would be midsummer madness to turn back to the theories of the Old South, if it were within the limits of possibillity to do so. Even South Carolina would not now return to slavery if it could. A large majority of her white leaders, and an overwhelming majority of the white people, would vote and battle against the restoration of black bondage. They would be glad to limit their prerogatives of citizenship, as would the people of Pennsylvania under like circumstances; but their inherent pride of State forbids it, although fully possessing the power, because it would dwarf the Commonwealth in the councils of the nation and rank her with the insignificant States of the Union. In the free mingling with the representative men of the Carolinas, including white and black, I have heard no hope or wish or fear expressed as to reactionary movements in those States. In South Carolina, where secession was part of school education more than half a century ago, and where the stern patriotism of a Jackson was needed to prevent nullification from breeding sectional war before many of the actors of the late war were born, there is no shade of a shadow of reactionary movement; and the man who attempted it would be hopelessly over-thrown. To assume that they have forgotten their love for their lost cause; their veneration for its heroes, their reverence for its dead, and their sorrow for its failure, would be to assume that they are more or less than human; but that they are thoroughly assimilated with the new duties that new occasions have prescribed, and are in sincere and hearty accord with the new hopes and new achievements which now invite them, is the honest truth. It can no longer be a matter of speculation, as the revolution in national power has thoroughly tested the aims and efforts of the Southern people, and they put to shame reckless demagogues who have fanned the embers of sectional strife long years after the defeated and im-poverished South has been struggling only for the right to retrieve its countless misfortunes.

It is startling to compare the growth of Virginia with the Carolinas since the war. It is true that Virginia bore more than her share of the brunt of the battle, as her territory is crowded with historic fields of sanguinary conflict and much of her lands were laid waste; but her loss by war was not more than the loss of South Carolina, and not so much considering the value of emancipated slaves. Virginia never drank the bitter dregs of carpet-bag rule, and her credit was never wasted by the profligacy of political adventurers. She never had a dollar of debt, outside of the universally rejected Confederate obligations, that was not the creation of the Old Dominion in the exercise of her own proud and deliberate authority. To-day Virginia is the only State in the South that has repudiated her own debt created by her own white people before the war, and she is in the rear of both the Carolinas in the growth of legitimate industry, business, and wealth. But if Virginia escaped the desolating tread of the carpet-bagger, she has inflicted upon herself a wound scarcely less vital than the worst of wounds which yet scar the other reconstructed States. When she should have profited by her naturally advantageous relations with the capital and industry of the North, and could have made her mountains, so richly studded with wealth, and her vast water-powers, so easy of access, fruitful sources of enduring prosperity, she

turned upon herself with suicidal hands, thrice repudiated her thrice accepted debt, effaced honor from
the jewels of the once proud Commonwealth, and
made capital and industry and integrity shun her
as the valley of death. She will grow and yet be
prosperous and great in spite of herself, but she
should to-day be in the front of Southern growth,
instead of lagging behind the States which had to
recover from the double curse of war and of the
empire of theft. North Carolina is now single from
the other reconstructed States in having attained,
solely by the efforts of her own people, a higher
degree of general prosperity than was ever before
attained in her history. She has a more prosperous
and thrifty people to-day than at any period of the
past, and there is more capital employed and less
debt, State and individual, than at any time in the
last half-century. Texas has surpassed the old
North State because of her large influx of immigration and wealth; but North Carolina has fewer
foreigners and a more completely homogeneous
population than any other State of the Union.
Since the rescue of the State from the tempest of
profligacy that swept over it after the war under
the Holden government, the taxes have steadily

diminished until they are only nominal, and the
schools have increased until they proffer education
to every child in the Commonwealth, regardless of
color. Her legitimate debt is steadily reduced; her
treasury has a large surplus; her humane institutions, conducted with equal care and outlay for
both races, are monuments of credit; her public
improvements have kept pace with the growing
wants of her people; her authority reflects the
pride of the State in its stainless integrity, and
thrift and content are the common blessings of her
people.

For this exceptional record there are many able
and true men to whom North Carolina is indebted;
but it is no injustice to any to say that to no one
is she so much indebted as to Thomas J. Jarvis, the
late Governor. His term of six years, ended only
by the mandate of the Constitution, has brought
the State to the largest measure of prosperity ever
known in all her past, and there is not a son of
North Carolina who does not share in the general
pride of a more than rehabilitated Commonwealth.
When it is considered that North Carolina has every
important mineral within her borders, from gold
to iron; that she has every variety of soil for every

variety of crops, from wheat to cotton; that she
has every variety of climate, from the sunny
Southern coast to the chills of the highest peak
of the Appalachian range; that she has water-power
enough in a single river to spin and weave the
whole cotton of the South, and that her lands are
nearly as cheap and her climate better than the
West,—when these facts are weighed in the scale
of intelligence, the momentous meaning of a New
South, with sectional tranquillity assured, may be
understood in the North as it is now understood
in the Carolinas. And South Carolina is little
behind her sister. Georgia doubtless ranks next
to North Carolina in the race for recovered prosperity, but South Carolina is close upon the heels
of both, and with graver obstacles to overcome.
Her loss in property by the war, including the
property value of slaves, was greater in proportion
to the population than that of any State in the
Union, and the very refinement of carpet-bag theft
and humiliation was reserved as her destiny. She
had not only the graver problem to solve of an
overwhelming majority of the most ignorant blacks
suddenly clothed with every attribute of citizenship, and with scarcely the shadow of property or

appreciated responsibility, but she had the deepest-rooted Southern sectionalism to master and the teachings and traditions of generations to unlearn.

But the Palmetto State has made the grandest progress during the last eight years, and omitting wealth reckoned for slaves, she is richer to-day than ever before, and with abundant evidence that the era of development, of intelligent business progress, and of rapidly multiplying wealth is just beginning its great work. It is naturally the richest planting and agricultural State of the whole Union, without any exception. It has the best soil, with every advantage for its most profitable cultivation, of any part of the South; and the people who have been born upon it and who have lived in the luxury of superabundance and again felt the poverty of helplessness, are just now mastering the problem that a Yankee, compelled to lie awake at night to invent a method to get his pork and beans or pumpkin pie, would have mastered in an hour. There is no other part of the South except Florida where so little labor will produce so much, but with the richest uplands skirting the Blue Ridge, and with three-fourths of the State adapted to corn, South Carolina has ever been a buyer of bread. She should

have thrice her present population and be able to feed
it from her own fields without impairing her more
valuable crops of cotton and rice, and every pound
of her cotton could be more profitably spun and
woven on her own superabundant water-powers, than
any other place on the continent. The New South
whispers of these achievements, and that is why the
sister Carolinas are more hopeful and more prosperous to-day than at any time since they summoned
the angel of sorrow to shadow the land.

COLUMBIA—SOUTH CAROLINA.

COLUMBIA was the favored city of the South before the war. It was the special pride of South Carolina, and South Carolina was the special pride of the whole distinctive Southern sentiment. It is a vast village of old-time planters' homes, with their heartsome shades, large verandas, wide halls, climbing flowers and vines, and with the live-oak to cool the streets and the ever-blossoming magnolia to perfume the atmosphere. Its broad avenues, excepting on one short business street, are almost forests of green shade in summer, and winter is softened into our Northern spring. Until Sherman came with vengeance in his track, there was no more beautiful city on the continent; but the healing of twenty years has not restored the savage waste of war. Blackened and crumbling piles of what once were attractive homes or public edifices yet remain in isolated instances as monuments of the fearful atonement the cradle of disunion has made for rebellion against the Republic. Nor was the destructive march of Sherman the greatest of South Carolina's calamities. After him came the scourge of the carpet-bagger, and for nearly a decade he revelled in the luxury of the thieving spoiler; and it was not until the cup of humiliation had been drained to its very dregs that the long dream of Southern omnipotence and of a Southern Confederacy vanished like a hideous phantom. Half a century ago the dream of the dismemberment of the Republic and the erection of an independent Confederacy, to be governed by the distinctly defined ruling class, and to be sustained by the distinctly defined servile producing class, first mingled with the slumbers of the Palmetto State, and thenceforth it was the disunion leaven of South Carolina that leavened the whole South and prepared it for the bloody achievements and failures which culminated at Appomattox in 1865. Notwithstanding the apparently crushing blow that Jackson gave to Calhoun and nullification fifty years ago, disunion was taught with ceaseless, subtle energy, and it was here that the first secession ordinance was passed, and it was in the harbor of South Carolina that the first hostile gun was fired at the flag. The assault and capture of Fort Sumter

made Columbia wild with rejoicing; the sequel came
when the flames kissed each other from home to
home and street to street as Sherman passed, and
the bondman became the ruler of the proud Palmetto
planters.

A painful history may be studied by a walk around
the ideal capital of the South. Long before the war
it was the hope of South Carolinians that separation
from the North must come sooner or later, and that
Columbia would be the capital and centre of Southern power. It pervaded not only the lordly planters
who had their troops of docile slaves, but the poor
white man, who struggled in ignorance and poverty
by the side of the often more favored bondman,
caught the inspiration of his superiors, and how
stubbornly he maintained it was fearfully attested on
many battle-fields. Like the scarcely understood
hope of the Russian serf, that his people must one
day worship at the cradle of the church in Constanti-
nople, the white serf of the South was enthused with
the no better understood hope of worshipping Southern omnipotence at the cradle of disunion in South
Carolina. It was this dream that founded the unfin-
ished capitol in this city. While planned ostensibly
as the capitol of South Carolina, on a scale of gran-

deur worthy of Greece or Rome in their best days, it was the unwritten law and the unconfessed hope of the State that the Palmetto capitol must be worthy of the future Confederacy as the temple of its laws, and for years before the clash of disunion arms was heard, the expected capitol of the slave empire was patiently progressing. It is colossal in size, and it was conceived in a degree of architectural magnificence before which every State capitol in the Union paled into obscurity. It had been raised to the square, ready for its richly ornamented copings and roof, when war arrested its construction, but enough had been done to portray its marvellous elegance. On the exquisitely carved marble facings of the four fronts of the building are hewn niches for the statues of the fathers of the new Confederacy, and artistic circles for commemorating in bas-relief those who deserved distinction above their co-laborers. But two of them are finished, and they present the profiles of McDuffie and Hayne; and who will fill the many vacant places, now that the whole dream has perished, some future generation must decide. In the poverty and desolation wrought by war and carpet-bag profligacy, there is no hope for the completion of this imposing structure by those now in

active control of the State. The era of severe economy has of necessity followed the desolating tread
of the adventurer, and the unsightly picture of dilapidation and waste is presented by the building that
was once the pride of every South Carolinian. The
beautiful walls are stained and their seams opened by
the ceaseless ravages of time, and the rude temporary
finish made under the reign of the stranger, to echo
the voice of the slave as he enacted laws for his
master, adds to the general dreariness that surrounds
Capitol Hill. Fluted or half-finished columns of imposing dimensions are scattered about the grounds;
elaborately wrought massive granite caps are rusting
beside the walls which await them, and the débris of
the finest Italian marble tells the story of the magnificence that was designed for this central altar of
Southern worship. Two monuments stand in the
unbecoming rudeness that surrounds them. One
tells how the North and the South once fought under
the same flag in Mexico, by an elegant bronze pal-
metto-tree, on which is engraved the fallen heroes
who overthrew the legions of Santa Anna, and the
other, "erected by the ladies of South Carolina," tells
in mute but eloquent marble how the Confederate
warrior braved and died for his cause.

There is no State in the South that has more thoroughly learned the true lesson of the war than South Carolina. It has all of Southern pride surviving its sorrow and desolation; the traditions of its people are as sacred as ever, as they must be with men who are worth national fellowship. It is not a convert to the wisdom of free labor or the enfranchisement of freedmen; but it does thoroughly understand that the traditions and customs of the past belong to the past, and that civil rights are as sacred for the lowly as for the mightiest in the land. The two races are more nearly in harmony in South Carolina than in any of the other slave States, and I believe that there is more kind feeling for the colored man, as a fellow-citizen, in this State than in any of the border States. Wade Hampton made the first successful experiment in dividing the colored vote in 1876, and that ended the rigid colored line in South Carolina. The colored leaders and their fellow carpet-baggers had plundered the Commonwealth, impoverished both whites and blacks, and the helpless freedman turned to the plantation and to his old master for corn and bacon as a deliberate and wise choice of evils. Since then, with the exception of the coast region, there has been as cordial harmony and mutuality of in-

5

terest, in both politics and business, between the whites and blacks, as is common in communities of one race, and the men who are ruling the State to-day are as jealous of the rights of the colored people as they are of their own. Schools have been multiplied in every county with the most scrupulous equality of educational advantages between the races; over eleven hundred colored teachers are now teaching in the colored schools in the pay of the State, and Democratic colored Representatives represent white constituents.

While the general harmony of the two races is assured in South Carolina, there is one black cancer on the sea-coast that is a fearful hindrance to the advancement of the colored race, and a fearful temptation to intimidation and fraud on the part of the whites. Beaufort has some six hundred white voters and more than as many thousand colored voters. If the colored population of that section was as intelligent as even the proverbially ignorant field-hands of the interior and upland sections, there would be some reasonable solution of the vexatious problem. If the rice and sea-island plantation negroes were the equal of their colored brethren in other portions of the State, they could assert their own rights with some

degree of intelligence; but they are the most hopelessly ignorant and debased of the race on the continent, and are incapable of improvement. They live
in the miasmas of the rice and island cotton plantations, where to tarry is often death to the white
man, and generation after generation have grown up
without intercourse with the whites, entirely without
facilities for culture, and they are ignorant to a degree that makes them incapable even of speaking
an intelligible language. They have the natural do-
cility of the negro, and they are like so many sheep
in the shambles for politicians on both sides. Sometimes they are rallied and voted indefinitely by unscrupulous leaders, as they defy individual recognition, and again they are terrorized by cunning .
Democrats, who well understand that a whisper to
the fears of these poor creatures makes them dream
of unspeakable horrors. This element is the only
one that is fraught with peril to both races in South
Carolina, and I have heard of no promising method
for correcting it; but South Carolina is about to open
on a long career of peaceful progress, in which the
whites and the blacks will advance together, and she
points to the sacredly maintained credit of the State,
to the premium commanded for her securities in the

Northern market, to the Democratic constitutional provision fixing free and equal education beyond the caprice of Legislatures, to the diffusion of industry by small tenantries, to the rapid increase of industrial products, and to the general tranquillity of all races and conditions of people, as conclusive evidence that there is a new South Carolina, with new duties honestly accepted, and with a new destiny of which the nation will soon be justly proud.

CHARLESTON.

THERE is no city on the continent that is more fragrant of song and story, or of field and forum, than is Charleston, the metropolis of the Palmetto State. Here Cavalier and Puritan were side by side in founding the new empire beyond the Western sea more than two centuries ago, and their altars remain among the noted landmarks of the earliest settlement. St. Philip's Church gathered its worshippers of 1681 to their devotions, and its two thickly-settled cemeteries, with their quaint and crumbling monuments to the dead, brightened by the magnolia, the live-oak, the evergreen, and the beauty and fragrance of perpetual flowers, make the romance of history lustrous. There, among the earliest sleepers of the colonists of the Lord Proprietors, fitly reposes the dust of Calhoun, whose square brick tomb, marked by a plain marble slab, is shaded by a large magnolia that stands as a central guardian of the dead of five generations. St. Michael's Church has heard the supplications of four generations, and its yet noted chimes summoned the multitude to prayer and praise half a generation before the Revolution. Its bells were taken by the British in 1782, shipped back to England as trophies of war, again bought and re-shipped in 1783, and rang out their sweet music from the old belfry until the black cloud of civil war came in 1861. They were so highly prized as living and speaking mementos of the founders of the proud Southern Commonwealth that they were shipped to the interior city of Columbia for safety, where they met the fury of Sherman's avenging army, and were made voiceless by the flames which desolated that beautiful capital. The tuneless metal was reshipped to England, recast in copy and quantity by the same establishment that had furnished them a century before, and in 1867 they rang out the same sweet chimes which had sung the first sacred belfry song of the Colonies. The Huguenots reared their altar two full centuries ago, and their church has twice been destroyed by fire; but its unmixed Gothic archi-tecture, neat finish, and many tablets in commemo-ration of its founders, as presented to-day, fully pre-pare the visitor for the fact that it is the only church on the continent that yet adheres strictly to the Huguenot worship.

Charleston is at once a city of energy and decay, but its energy is in the business channels, where it is most needed, and its decay is in its buildings, where coming thrift can one day arrest it. Its generally beautiful, balconied and pillared homes are externally faded and musty from neglect, but there is beauty even in the long untouched, moss-grown walls and venerable ornaments which tell the story of the strange sacrifices the people have suffered. In December, 1861, soon after civil war had begun its march of destruction, a fire swept over a large portion of the city and consumed six millions of property. The four years of desperate, deadly fraternal strife that followed gave no time or means to repair the waste, and when war ended in 1865 no community in the South was more exhausted or more desolated than this people that had been to the fore-front in inviting and precipitating the unnatural conflict. Nor did the return of peace open the way to retrieve the unspeakable misfortunes of war, for when the sword was sheathed and the flags of contending armies were furled, there came a visitation even more terrible and destructive than war. The adventurer, the thief, the carpet-bagger enthroned themselves in the chaos, and there was a decade of waste, demoralization, and paralysis that sapped the vitals of every resource and hope of the people. The proud patrimony of a great Commonwealth was ineffaceably stained with dishonor; the ignorant freedmen were publicly invited to despoil their former masters by theft and oppression, and for ten years the plunderers of high and low degree held ceaseless carnival amidst the hopeless poverty of every honest home. The whole machinery of government, including the Executive, the Legislature, and the Courts, was made the mere agent of adventurers to rob and shame the State, and popular elections were but a mockery of the voters. At last relief came in the memorable struggle of 1876, when peace was born in the throes of smothered revolution at Columbia, and the considerate student of the decade of carpet-bag infamy that deepened and widened the desolation and sacrifices of war, will judge in generous justice the passive assent to the electoral fraud of 1876 that gave South Carolina, Florida, and Louisiana home rule. It was thus fifteen years after the sorrows and sacrifice of war began, and ten years after the tread of hostile armies had ceased, that

Charleston began the work of rehabilitation, and even the presumably more energetic and versatile people of the North, with like prostration, wasted resources, and sluggish surroundings, would have progressed little if any better than has the city of Charleston. Instead of repining over the countless woes which befell them in the discomfiture of war, the emancipation of slaves, the destruction of wealth, and a revolution in popular government to which they were not only strangers, but trained to misunderstand, they have rapidly rebuilt their commerce, enlarged their industries, quickened their surrounding producers, and entered the race to regain their position and wealth with a heroism and steady endurance that have accomplished marvellous results. But it will require years to restore the thrift that reared the beautiful homes and churches and schools and other monuments of wealth and culture by which old Charleston marked her magnificent pro-gress, and there is pardonable decay in the external signs of the city while energy and growing advance-ment are visible in all the channels of business enter-prise. There is now unclouded peace and trust between the North and the South; the advent of a national revolution in politics has dissipated the last

hope of the partisan demagogue and the last fear of
the sensitive capitalist, as it has proved that with a
President elected by the solid vote of the South there
is thoroughly loyal devotion not only to the Union
but also to the irrevocable judgments of the war. If
the administration of Cleveland were to fail in all its
confidently expected governmental reforms, it would
still leave one priceless blessing to the whole nation
in the absolute and staple faith it has established
between the material interests of the two sections of
the country.

Standing on the Battery, with the vast expanse of
waters leading to the sea before you, and the most
attractive homes of the city flanking the little park
on the other side, Fort Sumter is visible nearly four
miles away, and its sister forts, remembered as Castle
Pinckney and Fort Moultrie, may also be dimly seen
in the distance; but all have ceased to have frown-·
ing battlements. Castle Pinckney has been trans-
formed into peaceful pursuits; Fort Moultrie remains
with its guns dismantled and its bulwark razed, and
Fort Sumter, about which crowd such a wealth of
historic memories, quietly nestles in the water midway between Morris and Sullivan Islands, without
sign of the grim purposes of war. Instead of the

batteries which belched forth their harmless shot and shell in obedience to the orders of Anderson, a light-house relieves the squatty summit of the memorable fortress to light the path of the commerce and wealth of peace. It was in this city that rebellion against the Nation had its birth; it was here that the first hostile gun was fired against the flag, and it was here that the last and saddest sacrifices of war were felt. The people of South Carolina are nothing if not heroic, and right or wrong, they are sincere, earnest, and brave. It was in Charleston that rebellion was organized againt the Lord Proprietors of King Charles in 1719; it was in Charleston that rebellion against King George began in 1774; it was in Charleston that rebellion attempted nullification of the revenue laws in 1831, and it was in Charleston that rebellion culminated in civil war in 1861. The heroic qualities of the Cavalier and the Puritan have written these momentous chapters in the annals of American history, and the same heroic qualities are now leading in the restoration of the South to prosperity, and on a basis that must speedily give the reconstructed States a degree of substantial wealth and power that was never dreamed of before the war. On the 12th of April, 1861, when the first gun was fired from Moultrie at Sumter, it was not only the proclamation of fraternal war, but it was the signal-gun of a political, industrial, and social revolution in the noblest and strongest government of the world. Like all such revolutions, it brought sad bereavements and fearful sacrifice. On the 18th of February, 1865, the next proclamation in the irresistible progress of the great revolution was made as the signal-gun of Sherman ordered the advance upon the then defenceless city. The next proclamation of the progress of the ripening fruits of the seed sown in the fierce tempest of battle was when Wade Hampton conquered anarchy at Columbia and joined his old battle-scarred friends and foes in the Senate, and now all the well-springs of fraternity, of peace, and of united energies are hastening the grand consummation. This history is impressed here on every side. The beautiful homes which dot the isle where once Fort Moultrie frowned; the mission of peace that has its altar on the crown of Sumter; the levelled intrenchments which once bristled with guns in the wide crescent of defences on the sea-side of the city; the Confederate monument that tells of the lost Moultrie, and divides the sympathies of the people with the equally beautiful monument of

Sergeant Jasper, who restored Moultrie's flag in the hottest of a Revolutionary battle, and the Confederate Home, where the maimed soldier who fought for the stars and bars, hoists and lowers the stars and stripes with rising and setting sun, all tell the story of the beneficent revolution that has been wrought, and of the inevitable grandeur and prosperity of the reunited American people. In no other nation of history could nearly two millions of brave reapers in the terrible harvest of death have been remanded to the channels of peaceful industry without a jar in government, commerce, or trade, and it is even a nobler tribute to the people of North and South that the soldiers of both the blue and the gray have been the manly conservators of peace and order since they retired from the conflicts of matchless heroism. There is peace and trust throughout the land; the scars of war are being fast effaced, and the new generation, with its new South and new North, will worship the most beneficent government and witness the most prosperous people of the earth.

GEORGIA—THE EMPIRE STATE OF THE SOUTH.

GEORGIA is the Empire State of the South. Nature made her so by a wealth of soil and mines that is unequalled in any of the coast or Gulf States south of Virginia, excepting Alabama, and her people have been proverbial for more than ordinary Southern progress. The blight of slavery has made her farms unsightly and hindered the development of her ruling class, but Georgia has ever been the conservative centre of the cotton region, and thrift and comfort have been more generally diffused here than in any of the other slave Commonwealths. There are more small farms than in any other part of the cotton region, and the local business centres wear a healthier aspect than is common in Virginia and the Carolinas, while Atlanta has every appearance of being the legitimate offspring of Chicago. There is nothing of the Old South about it, and

58

all the traditions of the old-time South, which are made poetical to dignify effete pride and logical poverty, have no place in the men of the present in the young and thriving Gate City. There must be old regulation Southerners in this region, but they have either died untimely in despair, or they have drifted into the current and moved on with the world around them. The young men are not the dawdling, pale-faced, soft-handed effeminates which were so often visible in the nurslings of the slave. They have keen, expressive eyes; their faces are bronzed; their hands are often the tell-tales of labor; their step is elastic and their habits are energetic. They bear unmistakable signs of culture; but it is the culture that came with self-reliance, and it is valued because it cost them sacrifice, invention, and effort. They have learned that "hardness ever of hardiness is mother," and if the young men of Georgia who have grown up since the war do not soon assert themselves and make a most whole-some shaking up of the old fossil ideas and dreams of the South, every present indication must prove delusive. With a city like Atlanta, that has not a vestige of old Southern ways about it, in the very heart of the State and the temple of her laws, it is simply impossible that such keen and powerful pulsations can fail to quicken the whole people. You hear no curses of the blacks from idlers in Atlanta. They understand that the negro is away behind them; that his future is a doubtful one, and they vote him and vote with him; open schools of all grades for him, on equal footing with the white; trade with him in politics and in business, and move on in their own way without leaving obstacles in the path of the black man or caring much whether he advances or falls in the race. They know that the negro will never rule the State or anything else; that he won't rule himself, and while really cherishing more sincere and practical kindness for him than most of those who bubble over with sympathy for him at long range in the North, they have no political or business warfare with him, and he votes as freely in Georgia as he does in Pennsylvania.

There are more potent civilizers in Georgia than I have met with in any other portion of the South, and they are not few in number. The more intelligent young men of from twenty to thirty years, who are now beginning to assert themselves, are, as a rule, the foremost missionaries in the new civilization in the South. They are fretful under the booted and spurred Brigadiers, who insist that the sons shall bear aloft the shields of their fathers, and make themselves mournfully sentimental over the Lost Cause. They are as reverent of their fathers as circumstances will permit, but they believe that the abolition of slavery was a blessing to the South as well as to the nation, and they don't believe in wailing about the loss of what they wouldn't have back if they could get it. They honor the graves and memories of those who fought and fell in the cause of the South; they build beautiful monuments to prove that they are not strangers to their parentage, but they feel that if their fathers had been half as heroic in developing the South and stamping it with peaceful progress as they were in fighting for what they never should have had, the Southern States would be a garden of beauty and plenty to-day. They are especially anti-Bourbon in politics, and a large majority of the more cultured and energetic young men of Georgia would to-day be Republicans from choice if Republicanism as now directed was not mainly a mixture of sectionalism and plunder. They don't want offices, for they have learned a better way of making a living, and

6*

they are manly in their independence. Instead of discussing the old plantation times "before the wah," they talk about railroads, factories, the tariff, the schools, the increase of crops, and the growth of wealth and trade, and these are civilizers which will soon disarm Southern Bourbons and Northern demagogues. The rapid growth of this new civilization is evidenced by the increase in number of small farmers and their general prosperity, and in the rapidly multiplied factories in both the cotton and iron sections of the State. With forty cotton-factories and the ceaseless hum of nearly two hundred thousand spindles, and with nearly one hundred furnaces and iron-mills to diversify industry and open new markets for the farmers, there must be progress. The factory and the school are the great civilizers of the age in the South, and they are now doing a grand work in Georgia. Here the cotton is grown; here labor is cheaper than in the North; here it can be fed and clothed better than on the bleak hills of New England or in the crowded cities, and here the cotton-spindle should answer the song of the cotton-gin. And wherever the factory is reared, there is a new civilization planted in the desolation of slavery. The shade,

the vine, the flower, the tidy fence, and the tasteful
home about the cotton-mill, tell the story of the
future South, and the uniform prosperity of the
mills of this State must speedily multiply their
numbers. They have invaded South Carolina across
the Savannah from Augusta, and Augusta has built
a vast canal to furnish water-power to invite capital, while South Carolina exempted from taxation
for ten years all factories erected in the State.*
Columbus, in this State, is one of the most prosperous towns in the whole country, solely because
of the many factories which nestle in and around
it, and some of the mills divide from fifteen to
thirty per cent. to their shareholders, while all of
them are earning profits. The Cotton States now
bring three hundred millions of dollars annually
to their people by their cotton crop, but they pay
the Northern and foreign mills nearly as many millions to spin it, when they could earn the nearly three
hundred millions more easily here than it can be
earned elsewhere. In short, their crop that is worth
three hundred millions when it comes from the

---

* The exemption law was repealed this year, but it still applies to
all erected under the law.

cotton-gin, would be worth six hundred millions if they turned it out from the spindle and loom, and they are just beginning to understand that simple question of arithmetic. The young men, the factory, the school, the hardiness and comfort of industry,— these are the new civilizers which are to revolutionize the old Slave States.

I am sorry to point to one blot on the escutcheon of Georgia that should be effaced. It is much the creation of the lingering passions of war and of the irritation and distrust of the rule that followed reconstruction. There were many unwise enactments under the Bullock administration, which had all the flavor of reckless profligacy. Aid was lavishly voted to speculative railways, and adventurous strangers expected to profit by them much more than they expected to profit the State; and there was natural revolt against the whole policy of the new government. Governor Bullock finally gave up the unequal contest by resigning; the projected railroads were mostly built in some way, and no venality has ever been traced to Bullock; but a sweeping tide of repudiation followed, and some six millions of apparently lawfully contracted debt has been refused payment. The accepted debt of the State is about nine

millions, but there is railroad property representing
it that would nearly or quite pay it at present market
value. There is, therefore, no plea of necessity to
excuse Georgia in repudiating any part of her debt;
but it has been consigned to repudiation, first by
statute and next by constitutional amendment in
1877, forbidding legislative appropriation for interest
or principal, and denying the courts jurisdiction to
inquire into its validity. This refusal to submit the
question of the legality of the debt to the judicial
tribunals of the State, all of which are in harmony
with the political power that repudiated the bonds, is
a confession that a dispassionate inquiry into the matter would be likely to sustain the claim of the creditors for at least part of the debt. By closing the
courts against the bondholders, Georgia has grievously wronged herself, and her people must revoke
the constitutional mandate of repudiation or stand
dishonored before the world. As thistles can't bear
figs, so repudiation can't bear anything but demoralization and wrong-doing. The repudiated bonds are
valueless on the market, and the false attitude in
which Georgia has placed herself tempts the speculator to trade in her dishonor. Counsel for the
bondholders, representing those who hold at little

cost, are besieging Congress to open the United States Courts, by constitutional amendment, and invite suits against the States by individuals. Such amendment is fraught with such boundless evils that it can't prevail; but it is one of the many pretexts for sectional turbulence, and for unscrupulous politicians and speculators to seek Congressional aid to force the South into submission. It is not done against Republican Minnesota, but it is done against reconstructed Georgia. If it were a wise thing to do, it should be done without regard to North or South, but neither section will accept such an amendment of the Constitution when they must look it squarely in the face. The new Georgia that the new civilizers are rapidly fashioning should open her courts to her creditors, as they are now open to all citizens to test the validity of debts, and I believe that before another decade shall have passed every debt that has been unjustly repudiated will be honestly assumed and paid.

The race question is not a serious problem in Georgia, as is shown by the harmony that exists between the whites and the blacks, and by the wonderful growth of wealth among the blacks. When Governor Bullock retired from the office, the assessed property of the blacks in the State was not one hundred thousand dollars, and now, under the same assessment laws, it is many millions. The negroes have become large purchasers of small cotton farms, and they have prospered beyond all reasonable expectation. This class of blacks are not politicians by trade, and most of them vote with the many reputable white Republicans in the State for the Democratic State and local tickets, although they maintain their Republican faith and organization. They do not want the class of State and legislative officers that Republican local rule would inevitably bring upon them. They have just laws, equal protection for both races, economical government, universal education, and they want no change. In Atlanta one-sixth of the whole voters are white Republicans, but most of them vote steadily for Democratic State and local rulers. The schools of the State are open to both races on equal terms, and the State aid to the colored college has been placed on exact equality with the State University for whites by constitutional provisions. High schools, equally for both races, may be maintained by special county taxation, if ordered by a vote of the people, and two high grade schools specially for the colored race are in progress in At-

lanta, exclusive of the colored college. This general
system of education, equally for both races, has not
been grudgingly adopted by the white government of
Georgia. On the contrary, it is heartily sustained by
the great mass of the whites, and, as a rule, they gen-
erously aid rather than hinder the advancement of the
blacks. The healthy divisions between the whites
on State and local tickets have made all sides seek
friendly relations with the blacks, and not one of the
many more intelligent colored citizens I have met
has complained of any want of justice to their race.
But for the stain of repudiation that rests upon
Georgia, I would say that her people have been as
conspicuously faithful as they have been prosperous in revising her citizenship and rehabilitating
the Commonwealth.

Atlanta ranks with Richmond and Vicksburg
in historic associations connected with the war. It
did not differ greatly from other Southern cities
before Sherman destroyed it, but it had become a
great railway centre, and as such was a most important military base for either army. It was more
heroically defended by the Confederacy than any
other point, with the single exception of Richmond,
and no one city of the South witnessed such desper-

ate conflicts immediately around it for its possession. With all the exceptional growth of Atlanta and the wonderful repairs of the ravages of war, there are vastly greater evidences of the sanguinary struggle here than at the Confederate capital, for the capture of which there was such fearful sacrifice of life. The battle for Atlanta was immediately around Atlanta, and the earth-works on which Hood made his last desperate and bloody stand for this gateway to the vitals of the South, are yet to be seen in broken fragments about the beautiful residences which embellish the suburbs of the city. Here the last hopeful struggle of the South was made, for after Atlanta fell there never was anything like an equal battle fought between the two armies. Thomas crushed the remnant of Hood's veterans at Nashville, and Grant simply hastened the overthrow of Lee rather by wearing out than by open conflict. A beautiful monument but a little distance from the city commemorates the heroism and lamented death of the gallant McPherson, and every acre of ground in and for miles around the city has felt the shock of the most valiant armies of the world and has been the death-couch of the blue or the gray. When Sherman entered it with his shattered but

7

victorious army he was in the heart of the enemy's country, and the destruction of the city was deemed a military necessity. Hood had destroyed all the buildings containing any stores before he retreated, and Sherman accepted the harsh necessity of destroying the place to leave the enemy without a base to reorganize and pursue him in his perilous march to the sea. He notified the citizens to elect which government they would choose for their protection, sent those who gave the oath of allegiance to the North, gave all others safe-conduct beyond his lines, with such property as they could take with them, and then made Atlanta one scene of desolation. Here and there an ante-bellum Southern home stands in contrast with the modern buildings which surround them, but they were as brands snatched from the burning. Atlanta was destroyed, but it remained the gateway of the trade that survived the waste of war; it is on the through line from the North to the Gulf; the best vigor of the South with the best vigor of the North seem to have met here on the same mission, and the new Atlanta is the Queen of Beauty among Southern cities and is rich in all that constitutes enduring wealth.

The influence of Atlanta upon Georgia and upon the whole South is incalculable. Already it has revolutionized Georgia. It has not been done by Atlanta verdicts at the polls so much as by the advanced leadership that pours out its live currents of healthy progress in every direction. There are Confederate fossils here as elsewhere in the South, but their wails fall upon heedless ears; they are placemen who flaunt the Republican flag bearing the skull and cross-bones of sectionalism, but there are many reputable business men of the Republican faith who will one day reach a better domination for the party, and there are many thriftless negroes who steal and sell their votes to both sides and cheat all around in every election contest, but there are solid colored men in trade, and the colored college keeps abreast with the white university in the higher education of the black man. Here the most advanced leaders of the whole South have their homes, and they are felt in every precinct of Georgia, and the tide of progress cannot be swelling up in the centre of the South without overflowing and finding its outlet into all the surrounding States.

The bold deliverance made by Senator Brown

before his election to the Senate, undoubtedly voiced the purposes of the new Atlanta and of the new South. He had no Confederate scars to commend him to the Bourbons. On the contrary, he had vexed Jefferson Davis with threatened secession from secession when the war struck Georgia, over which he then ruled as Governor, and he was the chosen Chief Justice of the Bullock Republican reign and a Grant delegate to the Chicago Convention in 1868. He is consistent and logical, therefore, in his pointed declaration that Georgia must move as the world moves, and he was chosen to the Senate over General Lawson, one of the most distinguished of Confederate soldiers, with all his past record to offend the Bourbon South and solely because he has shaken off the musty shroud of the Confederacy, left the dead to sleep with the dead, and proposed to advance to the living present with heroic intent to deliver the reconstructed States from the gloom and poverty of the past. With Georgia, the mightiest and most prosperous of all the Southern States, thus asserting herself in favor of what is to be the new civilization of the South, I look for her to be more potential in the restoration of the South to enduring prosperity than any other factor in solving the great problem known as the Southern question.

Atlanta is fairly typical of Georgia in the solidity of her prosperity. It is not the apparent prosperity that is visible "where wealth accumulates and men decay." It is the general diffusion of wealth and the diffused creation of individual wealth for its own producer that makes Georgia exceptionally prosperous to-day, and the same causes are producing like results largely in South Carolina and in North Carolina. Necessity broke up the immense plantations of Georgia, and what her planters deemed a dire calamity several years after the war has proved the greatest blessing to her people. The attempts made for several years after peace to renew cotton-growing on the old plantation system bankrupted a large majority of the planters. They did not understand free labor, free labor would not understand the old plantation ways, and when the planters gave up in despair, the small farmers, white and black, rented little slices of the plantations, prospered as their own employers, gradually purchased small homes, and now both laborer and planter are growing rich together. It is not the wealth and luxury of the old-time plantations, but it is the better and more

7*

enduring wealth and comfort that comes from well-directed industry and the harmony of all classes. I believe that in another decade Georgia will have doubled her cotton production; that her own bread will all be grown on her own soil, and that the income from her cotton will be doubled from every bale by spinning and weaving her entire product. An adjustable attachment to the cotton-gin is already in use that takes in the raw seed-cotton and turns it out in yarn, thus doubling the market value of every pound; and with the impetus given to the spindle and the loom in Georgia, it is not an extravagant assumption to say that the growth of cotton will be nearly doubled in another ten years in Georgia, and that Georgia spindles will double the value of the doubled product. Every good cotton crop, under the direction of small farmers, is certain to increase the succeeding crop by the improvement of the land and the enlargement of the planting, and the opportunity for both is immense in all the cotton States. So far from being surprised at the wonderful increase of wealth in the South during the last ten years, the only surprise to the intelligent student of Southern opportunities and possibilities is that a people prompted by necessity, as the South has been, did not much more increase their wealth. Unless some new hindrance to Southern progress shall be invented by those who have everything at stake in sectional turbulence, the census of 1890 will show a growth in every element of prosperity in the South that even the progressive North cannot equal.

The city of Augusta, just across the Savannah from South Carolina, is one of the most attractive cities of the South, and it has many things besides its broad, shaded streets and towering cotton-mills to attract the visitor. The tallest smoke-stack ever erected in the country stands at the edge of the city, as a monument of solitude to tell of the vast Confederate powder-works which were once a hive of industry there. The powder-works have all disappeared, but the tall smoke-stack stands and towers high over the city, with an inscription telling its own story. It has been dedicated as a monument, and is maintained in good condition by one of the Southern war associations. Close by an old, vine-clad church, whose city of the dead is washed by the waters of the Savannah, is the grave of the Bishop-General, Leonidas Polk, and by his side sleeps his wife; and in the centre of the broad street that divides the city is the most beautiful Confederate monument of the South,

excepting only the New Orleans monument of Lee.
But now peace has come with all its beneficent fruits,
and the hum of thousands of spindles and the clank
of hundreds of looms declare how Georgia is aiding
in the creation of the New South.

MONTGOMERY—ALABAMA.

MONTGOMERY is one of the old-time beautiful cities of the South. Its winter is perpetual spring, and the live-oak shades which beautify the homes on the gentle hills surrounding it are scarcely rusted in their summer verdure. On an eminence fronting a business street double the width of Broad in Philadelphia, stands the Capitol, and from its white portals there is a grand view of the city and the surrounding country for miles. The highlands are green with the shades of the massively-pillared residences which denote the luxury and culture of old plantation days, and below is the silver line of the Alabama as it lazily drifts to the sea. There are evident signs of the dark days which befell the South and of the countless sacrifices which came with them. With twenty years of peace and half as many years of slow revival of wealth, there are unmistakable evidences of the yet unarrested decay that began when poverty followed war. I can

77

readily imagine what Montgomery was twenty-five
years ago, when it witnessed the most imposing civil
pageant in the history of the Confederacy, in the
inauguration of its Provisional President. The Capital of Alabama had been chosen as the Capital of
the new Confederacy, and the greenest of Southern
laurels and the happiest smiles of Southern beauty
welcomed the first civil ruler of the Slave Republic,
as he was borne through the streets by eight elegantly caparisoned horses, to receive the oath of office
on the portico of the first temple of Confederate laws.
There were then no shadows to mingle with the enthusiasm of the blindly rushing multitude. There were
no vacant chairs about home circles, no bereavement
sobbing in Northern and Southern hearts. The Confederacy was here regarded as an accomplished fact,
and war was pronounced the hallucination of the
alarmist and dreamer. Beauty and bounty were on
every side in the new Capital, and the faded Executive Mansion that still nestles in its wealth of heartsome shade and flowers in the centre of the city, was
then typical of the beauty of its surrounding Southern
homes. Now the grinding wear of desolation and
want which came with disaster to the cause that here
was launched upon the boisterous sea of nations, is

yet visible even in the largely restored prosperity that has been attained in nearly half a generation of peace, and Montgomery is wonderfully beautiful with all her scars.

Alabama is rich in natural resources, rich in products, and richer in Bourbonism than is best for her people. There is peace among all races and classes, but it was long the peace of decay rather than the peace of progress. The whites have a majority of voters in the State, but the color line has passed away, and the control of the colored vote is more complete in Alabama with less violence or friction than in any of the other cotton States. The large masses of negroes are huddled together in the narrow cotton belt that crosses from west to east. There they outnumber the whites three and sometimes five to one, while in the other portions of the State they are in hopeless minorities. In the Capital county they are two to one, but they have their Democratic organ owned and edited by a colored man; they have their Democratic clubs in which many of the most thrifty and intelligent negroes are active members, and they fairly give the whites a majority against their own race simply because the stench of carpet-bag and colored rule is yet in their nostrils, and because every business interest is identified with white control. As I write I can see from the window the broad street crowded with the rude vehicles of the colored tenants who are hurrying their cotton crop to market to "get straight" with their rent. Many of the fields are yet white with their fleecy harvest, but swarms of the tenantry are to be seen in the street daily with their rickety wagons, lank mules, and rope harness, but every bale of cotton is fifty dollars of wealth, and the colored tenants are rapidly acquiring riches. A large renter informed me that what are known as "rent notes" of colored tenants are among the best collaterals in the loan of money, and better than the same obligations of white renters as a rule, because the negro who summons up the energy to farm for himself is reasonably certain to succeed, and his first effort is to pay his rent. Blacks and whites are indiscriminately intermingled on the street, at the cotton stores, and in all the channels of business, and the shops and other mechanical pursuits exhibit the white and the black man side by side in earning their bread. Thus on the surface there is colored thrift and harmony between the races, but Alabama is behind Georgia and even South Carolina in solving the great problem of the

South. Her people were left richer at the close of the war than the people of any of the Southern States. They had large stores of cotton to throw into market at an enormous price, and the destructive tread of contending armies was unfelt outside of Mobile and the narrow line of Wilson's raid. They had not necessity as the stern teacher of progress as Georgia, the Carolinas, and Virginia had, and their old plantation system is preserved in the cotton belt, and a negro tenantry is making wealth for the planters. The schools are open in every township equally to both races; graded schools are maintained for both in the larger towns and cities, and two normal schools for the blacks are sustained by the State; but negro suffrage is here more than in any other region I have seen the dependence of the whites. Much of it is due to the fearful fraud practised upon them and the State by the infamous carpet-bag rule of six years, as it impoverished whites and blacks alike and left the deluded negro politicians demoralized and starving; but there is a measure of absolute dependence upon the whites by the blacks that is not common in the South. They have learned that the whites will rule; they know that they and their property are safer with home judges and planter jurors, and they are easily controlled in politics when a color line would at best be hopeless. I believe that the intelligent colored driver who took me through the beautiful city summed up the race issue in a single sentence. When asked whether they were intimidated in voting, he answered, "De gen'men don't do it; but dere's right smart of it among de low-down folks." Between the planters and their old slaves there is the kindest feeling and generally sympathetic relations, but in desperate political emergencies "de low-down folks" are important factors in effecting results.

Alabama has had her full proportion of the carpet-bag scourge in profligate waste and dishonest multiplication of debt under color of law, and this is the only State whose Democratic administration, that was chosen to correct the ways of the plundering adventurer, made the carpet-bag government comparatively respectable by imitating its misrule. The lavish expenditure of public money under the early reconstruction government and the wild abuse of the credit of the Commonwealth utterly bankrupted the treasury, closed the public schools for more than a year, flooded the country with temporary loan bills receivable for taxes, and so completely destroyed all faith in the obligations of the State that the old and never disputed eight per cent. bonds of Alabama sold as low as twenty cents on the dollar. And when the people elected Governor Lindsay as a representative of the property interest, he became the victim or confederate of the old plundering régime, and left the office without retrieving the credit of the State. Abler and truer men succeeded him, and after much tribulation in both finding the whereabouts and extent of the debt, and in negotiating with the creditors, the obligations of Alabama have been funded in one class of bonds, bearing two, three, four, and five per cent. as they approach maturity. The carpet-bag rulers did not even keep a complete record of the debt they created or of the bonds they issued, and search had to be made in London, New York, and among the various railroads which were presumably aided by legislation, to ascertain how many millions of obligations were out bearing the promise of the State to pay them. A commission was created to hunt up and adjust the debt on some equitable basis for the approval of the Legislature, and after its final adjustment by sifting and compromise of the jobber's portion of it, there is now an accepted debt of nine millions, on which interest is promptly paid and gradual provision made for the payment of the principal. The debt question is, therefore, removed from the reach of agitation such as has convulsed and demoralized Tennessee, Virginia, and North Carolina, and there is assured stability in the integrity of Alabama.

MOBILE HARBOR AND RIVERS.

MOBILE is one of the few important natural gateways to the world of waters in the South, and second only to the Mississippi outlet in the industry it should inspire and the commerce it should command. The beautiful bay on which Mobile is situated has natural tributaries reaching far into almost boundless sources of natural wealth, which must at no distant day build up one of the grandest empires of the New South; and yet the Mobile of the present gives no token of its better destiny, and has only faded monuments of its past commerce and wealth. It teaches more pointedly than any other centre of trade in the South, the peril of a State that relies upon a single staple product and the peril of a city whose business is limited to a single productive industry. Before the war, Mobile handled eight hundred thousand bales of cotton annually, and that alone gave it a commerce that made it one of the most prosperous centres of the coast, with uncommon wealth, culture, and prosperity. The necessities of war quickened the energies of the South; new highways were opened for armies and for trade, and they diverted trade to new centres, leaving Mobile with two-thirds of her cotton shipments lost in the race. Cotton was the one staple product of Alabama, and the one source of the commerce of Mobile, and when cotton was attracted to other commercial centres, there was nothing left for Mobile but paralysis and decay. The same people remain the same; culture is maintained in its proverbially hospitable people; the same earnest, hopeful effort prevails in her intelligent business circles; but neither population, culture, nor business effort can succeed in the unequal contest that has confronted that city of such exceptional natural advantages, and the unerring index of departed business and thrift are noted in the tenantless temples of commerce and in the blighted chaplets of commercial achievement. The natural conclusion that would be accepted by the North is, that Mobile must be the author of its own decline; but it is not the truth. The war left this city impoverished as it left the South generally, and the vast outlay necessary to make the marvellous natural advantages of the port available has not been within the power of either Mobile or Alabama.

To understand the causes which have left Mobile without advancement for twenty years after peace, and appreciate the future possibilities of this city, it is necessary to take a comprehensive view of the State of Alabama. I have studied the resources and opportunities of the State with special. interest, because they are certain to revolutionize some of our chief sources of wealth in Pennsylvania; and the more they are studied, the more clear it must become to every intelligent mind that England is not to-day more the rival of the Keystone State in the future production of iron and coal than is Alabama. There is not a source of mineral wealth in Pennsylvania, excepting only our oil product, that is not found in Alabama in equal or greater abundance, with the matchless advantages of climate, of easier and cheaper production, and of vastly cheaper transportation. Nature's great gifts to Pennsylvania have been not only liberally supplemented in Alabama, but to them have been added every possible natural advantage for their cheap development and delivery to the markets of the world. If half the capital and business direction that have been given to make Pennsyl-

vania peerless in the production of mineral wealth
had been given to Alabama, her productive wealth
would be as great as that of the iron State, and her
population would be nearer five millions than the million and a quarter now scattered over the boundless
but almost untouched riches of this sunny Commonwealth. Think of a State with over five thousand
square miles of productive coal-fields, whose coal is
now sold at a fair profit in New Orleans at less than
four dollars per ton. It is mainly of the best quality,
alike for commercial, manufacturing, and domestic
purposes; it is in large veins; it is more easily mined
than our most favorably located bituminous coal-
fields in the North; and in large portions of the coal-
fields there is good iron in abundance, much of it
requiring no actual mining at all, and with the iron
and coal is found the limestone. What has been
done in Birmingham not only can be done as well in
many other parts of the State, but it can be even
more profitably done in Birmingham and elsewhere in
Alabama as soon as the great natural highways of
the State shall be made available; and no citizen of
the North of fair intelligence can review the slumber-
ing wealth of Alabama and the water-ways which
offer the cheapest transportation, without accepting

the conclusion that the next generation will see this
State an iron and coal centre equal to if not sur-
passing Pennsylvania, and Mobile the great coal
depot of the coast. It is this rational hope to which
this balmy city of the South clings in portraying the
revival of her commerce, the renewal and enlargement of her business temples, and the more than
restoration of her lost wealth and grandeur.

Not a vessel graces the broad rivers of Pennsylvania beyond the coast in the east. The Susquehanna, the Schuylkill, the Delaware, and the Juniata
are simply beautiful but useless outlets for our mountain springs as they go murmuring to the sea; but
Mobile is the outlet of many rivers which penetrate
into the leading centres of wealth in Alabama, and
the finest bay of the continent connects them with the
great highways of the world. With no more expenditure than has been wasted on mud creeks and summer mountain streams in a single River and Harbor
appropriation bill, the Alabama River could be made
navigable through the heart of the State away up to
Rome, in the northern part of Georgia, and the now
easy navigation of the Tombigbee could be extended
up the Warrior to the great centre of iron and coal,
west of Birmingham. No State not reached by the

Father of Waters and its tributaries approaches Alabama in the magnificence of her natural highways, and even the Mississippi, although commanding tribute from two-thirds of the States of the Union, offers no such facilities for the interior development of any one State as do the water-ways of Alabama. An expenditure of from half to three-quarters of a million would make uninterrupted water navigation from the Warrior coal and iron region to the sea, and two millions more would make the Alabama bring the fruits of her fields and mines from the far north and northeastern part of the State, and draw upon Northwestern Georgia to swell the commerce of Mobile. The channel of Mobile Bay has been already greatly improved, and every foot of depth attained has held its own. The pressure of the new energies of the New South must hasten the needed improvement of these great natural gifts to the commerce of the South, and when the river arteries of trade and the channel of the bay shall have been completed, the development of wealth in Alabama must be exceptional if not unexampled in the history of our substantial progress. As early as the administration of the second Adams the importance of these water-ways was appreciated by the government, but Cotton was king; it met every apparent want of the South, and as there was no supreme necessity to press these improvements, they readily bowed to the more imperious demands of trade in other sections of the Union.

It is no idle dream that makes the people of the once prosperous but now languishing port of Mobile hopeful of a renewed and greatly increased commercial prosperity in the near future. I regard the extension of her wonderful water-ways and the needed improvement of the channel of the bay as vastly more legitimate and important than the Hennepin Canal. The one is the traditional and accepted policy of the government; the other is straining the most liberal ideas of legitimate public improvements by Congress; and both the rivers and the harbor have already been recognized in past appropriations as demanding the generous aid of the country. When completed, as I assume they must be at an early day, Pennsylvania must look to her laurels; but there is no sound public policy that can make the interests of one State seek to hinder the development of a sister State that may outstrip the hitherto successful in the race for development and wealth. Whenever Alabama can make cheaper iron than

Pennsylvania to supply the country, Pennsylvania must transfer the rude music of her forges to the Sunny South; and whenever Alabama can supply the world with cheaper coal than Pennsylvania, the world will buy of Alabama, and Pennsylvania capital and energy will not take pause over sentimental theories, but hasten to follow the larger profits of industry. With water transportation from the immense coal-fields of Alabama, and Mobile Bay completed for the largest shipping, no State in the Union and no nation of the world will be able to compete with this State in supplying the Gulf of Mexico, the West Indies, and Central and South America with coal. England now draws some four millions annually from those countries for coal, while the United States draws little more than a quarter of a million; and the supremacy of Mobile as a cotton centre would be more than restored. Mobile would be literally the great gateway to the waters of the world for the Southern coal trade if given the benefit of the gifts nature has bestowed upon her; and what interest or what section can assume to hinder so great a consummation? There are four thousand square miles of virgin pine forest, with large supplies of cypress and white-oak, which would be made marketable by these completed

water-ways, and the cotton belt of Alabama and Eastern Mississippi that sought Mobile before the war
produces over a million bales annually. These are
stubborn facts; facts which the people of Mobile are
worshipping as the early salvation of both city and
State ; facts which the people of Pennsylvania and of
the North must look in the face soon at the latest,
and the sooner the better. They foreshadow the
same mutations in industry, trade, and wealth which
have left their inexorable lessons on all ages and
peoples of the past, and I welcome them as certain
to give lustre to another of the many unpolished
jewels of the Republic.

One of the bright days of the Southern journey dates a visit to the home of Mrs. Willson,
among the many old-time beautiful residences which
are in the suburban part of Mobile. Few in the
North would know Augusta J. Evans as Mrs. Willson, but the name of Miss Evans is familiar to
all the lovers of literature in every section of the
country. Her fine old mansion is thickly surrounded
by live-oaks in perpetual verdure, a profusion of
shrubbery and camellia-trees, radiant with thousands
of bursting buds and blooming flowers. One tree
that has evidently been the object of special care,

9

bore full three thousand bright scarlet buds and
flowers on its exquisitely symmetrical branches, and
when in full bloom it must illumine the whole
neighborhood. The visitors were promptly admitted
and greeted by the distinguished authoress in the
hospitable style of the true Southern home. She
was neatly clad in pretty gingham costume, and her
welcome made all forgetful of formality. She lives
and moves in a vast bower of flowers, all planted
and nursed by her own hands, and she exhibits
them with all the pride and affection of a Roman
mother. Refreshments were served, and the one
vacant place at the table had a napkin-ring hold-
ing an exquisite white camellia. "That," said Mrs.
Willson, "is my husband's bouquet for to-day, and
he has never been without one at any breaking
of bread in our home since we were married, now
sixteen years ago." She discussed authors with
freedom but in generous kindness, and spoke sor-
rowfully of the decline in Southern literature caused
by the long trials and sacrifices of war. She inquired specially for Miss Brewster, of Philadelphia,
and said that she had lately written to her urging the
reprint of new editions of her books. "I read no
history of the war," she said, with the impressive

pathos that only a woman could exhibit. "The story is too sad to me and to those who saw its terrible sweep of destruction, to be rescued from forgetfulness." She filled the hands of her visitors with flowers and their hearts with love. She is a model Southern housekeeper, takes entire charge of her plants and grounds and Jersey cows and horses, besides finding leisure to make rapid progress in her new book. "I do it by having system," was her answer when asked how she managed to do so much. It was a pleasant hour, and it added another to the many specially memorable incidents of the journey in the South.

BIRMINGHAM—THE SOUTHERN IRON CENTRE.

IF you want to see an infant Pennsylvania, with all the vigor and go-aheadativeness of the· regulation American boy just ready to bounce out of long clothes into high-legged boots, come to Birmingham, in the heart of Alabama. It is Young America personified and improved. It has more push and better bottom than any suddenly created city on the continent, and it is a revelation to both North and South. Towns have sprung up as suddenly in the oil regions and in new mining camps in the far Western mountains, but they have perished as speedily as they were created. Birmingham has all the solidity of Pittsburg, or Reading, or Allentown, and it requires no labored investigation to learn that, matchless as has been the growth of this new-born city, it is yet in its infancy and certain to attain the earliest and most

vigorous manhood. Twelve years ago the solitude
of Birmingham was attested by a single ordinary
farm-house ; but two railways finally crossed each
other there, and this invited capitalists to investi-
gate the great coal, iron, and limestone beds of
Central Alabama. Stories had been long told of
them that were regarded as akin to fable, and when
peace came, and railways began to traverse the New
South, capitalists came to the little house on the
cross railways, planted their investments about it,
and now a city of nearly twenty thousand population, with boundless energy and more than common thrift, has begun the inevitable revolution in
the iron trade of the continent. Some idea of the
substantial growth of the city may be learned from
the valuation of property for taxable purposes in
the county of Jefferson, that was two millions in
1882 and nine millions in 1884. It has none of
the signs of heedless haste for temporary use exhibited in the new oil and mining towns. It has
one of the finest opera-houses in the South; its
residences rival the beauty of Atlanta homes; its
stores and business houses present all the best qualities of Northern energy and method, and its large
class of skilled operatives enjoy a measure of com-

fort that is exceptional in Southern industry. It is largely a Northern creation, but it is worthy of note how thoroughly the Birmingham Southerner keeps abreast with the Northerner in every channel of progress.

Twelve years ago the total coal product of Alabama was ten thousand tons a year; now nearly half that amount is sent to market each day, the total tonnage of 1885 being over one million five hundred thousand. Twelve years ago the total pig-iron product of the State was sixty thousand tons; now it is six hundred thousand. These two sentences speak volumes to the iron and coal interests of the whole country. Remember that while the increase noted in the iron and coal product covers a period of twelve years, to date the sluggish product of ante-bellum times, the chief growth has been in one-third of that period, and during a season of continued and steadily increasing depression in the iron and coal trade of the country. This marvellous growth has come in Alabama when the Philadelphia and Reading Railroad Company has been bankrupted by the prostration of the iron and coal industries of Pennsylvania; there has been uninterrupted prosperity here, while a large proportion of our Pennsylvania furnaces have been driven to idleness, and those that continued have, as a rule, been fortunate if they escaped actual loss. In like manner, the coal trade of this region has been reasonably prosperous, while many of our Pennsylvania operators have been bankrupted, and others have escaped bankruptcy by closing their mines. The condition of the coal trade in the North has been clearly portrayed by the almost constant strikes and disputes between employers and employed, each struggling for the little profit the business offered, while here there has been no interruption in the production of coal. Convict labor largely fills the channels of unskilled industry in the mines, but free labor is much better, and it more than holds its own even against the unequal competition. There must be great natural causes for this contrast between the iron and coal industries of this city and like industries in Pennsylvania, where a full quarter of a century has been devoted to the perfection of transportation lines and the cheapest methods of production. We certainly have solved that problem in our State. Capital has not been wanting; on the contrary, it has been lavishly supplied to make our coal and iron beds most profitable; but with

all the boundless resources of the North, this iron
and coal centre prospers while the same industries
in the North languish, and when the South is only
in the infancy of transportation facilities. And let
not the North be deluded with the idea that this
strange development in the heart of the South is
ephemeral. There has been no sudden local demand
and no specially fortuitous circumstance to create
a city here as if by magic. It has been done simply
because it can, with imperfect facilities for reaching
the markets of the country, more than rival our
chief iron and coal centres of the North; and with
that fact accepted, what must be the future of a
State that has the resources to multiply its Bir-
minghams almost indefinitely?

Unless all evidence and calculation are at fault, the
iron and coal of this region within range of cheap
production are practically inexhaustible. Birmingham is part of the great Black Warrior coal-field, that
contains over five thousand square miles of accessible
coal, and to it may be added the two hundred square
miles of equally good and accessible coal in the Ca-
haba field and one hundred and fifty square miles
more in the Coosa field. In addition to these, it may
be well to consider the five thousand three hundred

square miles of coal just south of the Tennessee.
These nearly eleven thousand square miles of coal
are practically one vast coal-field, capable of supplying the world with that commodity. As yet it is
not penetrated by water navigation, but when half
a million dollars or little more would open the great
Warrior coal-field to uninterrupted water highway to
every port of the world through Mobile Bay, how
long will it require the lesson of Birmingham to open
the grand water highways of Alabama to the illimit-
able wealth of her coal-fields? The maximum cost
of coal here is one dollar and twenty-five cents per
ton at the furnace doors. It is found in nearly hori-
zontal strata, and varies from six to one hundred and
fifty feet in thickness, the Warrior field, whence this
city is supplied, having the thickest veins. The iron
ore, that is mined and delivered cheaper than at any
of our great iron-fields of the North, is absolutely
exhaustless, and embraces the red hematite and the
brown ores, with a more than ample supply of limestone close at hand. Red Mountain takes its name
from its iron, and it is almost literally a mountain of
iron. It is estimated by official geological reports
that there are five hundred billion tons of iron in it
alone. These exceptional facilities for producing iron

and coal are increased by the more genial climate and
cheaper labor that must ever be obtained where both
fuel and food are cheapened by the absence of severe
Northern winters. This is the only iron centre as
yet developed that seems to offer the production of
iron at the minimum of cost, as it has every requisite
for iron in superabundance, and all attainable at the
furnace with the least outlay. The one drawback
that has hindered the appearance of Birmingham iron
in all our Northern markets is transportation; but
even with the disadvantages of costly freights, iron
from this city now successfully competes with Pennsylvania at home and in New York and New England. The Southern railways cannot afford the cheap
freights that the Northern lines can offer because of
their immensely larger traffic; but the South will
rapidly improve in its transportation lines; its improved transportation will rapidly develop industrial
products, and both will rapidly cheapen transportation until it approximates Northern rates. And when
comparatively cheap railway transportation shall come
to the iron and coal of Alabama, with water transit
by the Warrior and the Tombigbee Rivers to the sea,
who can measure the growth of those industries in
this State?

It is idle for Pennsylvania and other great iron- and coal-producing States to close their eyes to the fact that we have reached the beginning of a great revolution in those products. No legislation, no sound public policy, no sentiment can halt such a revolution when the immutable laws of trade command it; and the sudden tread of the hordes from the Northern forests upon ancient Rome did not more surely threaten the majesty of the mistress of the world, than does the tread of the iron- and coal-diggers of Alabama threaten the majesty of Northern iron- and coal-fields. I do not credit the common saying that iron can be produced here for nine dollars per ton. There are many here who will tell you so; but after careful inquiry in the most intelligent and reliable circles, I fix an entirely safe limit of average cost at eleven dollars and fifty cents. There is iron produced here at less than that cost; but eleven dollars and fifty cents is as just an estimate for Birmingham as seventeen dollars is for Pennsylvania; and it must be remembered that Pennsylvania has reached the minimum cost in the production and marketing of her iron, while Alabama can and will greatly cheapen the delivery of her iron in the great centres of the trade. And what is true of iron must be equally true of coal. They are twin-sisters, whose development must keep pace with each other. Nova Scotia will soon learn to fear Alabama more than the small tariff now imposed upon her imported coal, and instead of extorting double prices for bituminous coal, as she did in the early days of the late war, before protection had developed our Northern mines, she will find Alabama crowding both herself and Pennsylvania in the New England factories, and with the water-ways of the State perfected, even England will have to look to her laurels in the Central and South American States. These lessons come upon us plain as the noonday sun, and it is midsummer madness not to read them understandingly. We cannot war with destiny; we cannot efface the beneficent gifts of Him who leads the waters to the sea and sends them back in the dews and rains of heaven. Alabama has been gifted far beyond even our boasted empire of Pennsylvania, and only the Southern sluggard has hitherto given the race to the North. Now there is a New South, with new teachings, new opportunities, new energies, and manifestly a new destiny, and the time is at hand when a large portion of the great iron and coal products of the country which enter competing centres will be supplied cheaper from Alabama than from any State in the North. How Pennsylvania will solve the problem I do not assume to decide; but the logical result would be the transfer of the portion of the iron industry that can best prosper here from the North to the South, just as the spinning and weaving of the home consumption of cotton must soon come to the cotton-fields and the better water-power and climate which they furnish.

Three trunk railway lines cross each other in Birmingham City, giving it the best railway facilities of any interior Southern centre, excepting only Atlanta. These lines, extending by main routes to the Gulf, to the Coast, to the East, to the Lakes, and to the West, and reaching every part of the country by their connections and tributaries, furnish rare facilities for the development of the wealth that abounds here; and new and important railway lines are soon to be added to them. And when it is considered that as railway outlets multiply, the great water highway by the Warrior River will be hastened to completion, the business possibilities of this region would seem incredible to the North even when cautiously stated. Through the kindness of the Mayor and the President of the Board of Trade I was enabled to visit and thoroughly examine the great coal mines and iron establishments which have created Birmingham, and the universal activity and unerring signs of prosperous operations present a marked contrast with our coal and iron centres in the North. There is a furnace here on a farm that furnishes everything necessary to make iron,—the iron ore, coal, limestone, and sand; and the great beds of iron, coal, and limestone are in a radius of four or five miles. That these exhaustless sources of wealth in such close proximity must soon defy competition in the product of the ordinary iron I regard as no longer a doubtful problem, but it is yet doubtful whether the competition can extend to the better qualities of iron and to steel. The manufacture of steel has not been attempted as yet, and while it is claimed that it will soon be produced here at the same relative cost as iron, and equal in quality to the steel of Pennsylvania, I feel no assurance that it can be done at all. The faith of the iron men of Birmingham is so strong in its resources that they confidently claim everything for it possessed by any other iron district of the world, even to the blades of Damascus; but here, as elsewhere in all the world, there will be material limitations upon the perfection of iron products.

Just what this vast field of as yet untested wealth may produce will be known only when the rattling, rollicking iron infant hurries on toward manhood; but discounting Birmingham by all that is yet undiscovered as to variety of iron, it is the most inviting iron-field on the continent, with a coal trade in the near future that will be bounded only by the coal ports of the world; and another decade will likely see more than a hundred thousand population here, with the whole region dotted with hives of industry such as Birmingham is to-day. With the marvellous progress made here when stagnation prevailed in all the coal and iron centres of the North, what must be the strides of this industrial centre when prosperity comes to revive the same industries in Pennsylvania? This country will draw the young men of energy from the coal and iron mountains of Pennsylvania, just as the fertile prairies of the West have drawn the young men of energy from our Pennsylvania farms, and there is room for thousands of them, with better prospects of success than in any new State or Territory of the Union. These are strong expressions, but I write them only after the most exhaustive inquiry and careful examination, and I know that they are fully warranted. This is the coal and iron empire of the South, and, I believe, the future coal and iron empire of the United States; and it has a climate and soil adapted to the bountiful growth of everything grown in Pennsylvania, with one-sixth of the entire cotton crop of the South added. It is the equal of Pennsylvania in forest, field, and mine, with climate, natural highways, and cheapness of product turning the scales in her favor. These are stubborn truths, and let us profit by them. They will not make Pennsylvania poor, for her people and resources are equal to any and all the mutations of industry and trade; but they will make Alabama rich, and that will multiply the wealth and grandeur of the whole Union.

MISSISSIPPI.

THE capital city of Mississippi is a good-sized village of five or six thousand people, with a few rusted and ancient-looking streets which bear evidences of old-time wealth and present comfort. On the gentle undulations which surround the now muddy centre that clusters about the railroad there are many fine Southern homes, most of them only a single story in height, but with the stately pillars, broad halls and verandas, and shades and shrubbery, which declare the existence of hospitality and luxury. The venerable Capitol in which the supreme power of Jefferson Davis was felt for many years, graces the centre of the city, but its faded elegance adds little to the architectural beauty of the public and private edifices. Cotton is the chief staple of the State. There is a little wheat and corn growing in some sections, a little turpentine-tapping and lumbering, and a beginning at stock-growing and manufacturing, but cotton is the product that is relied upon. There should be a rapid increase of stock-growing, as the climate and natural grasses are specially favorable for the cheap and good care of cattle, and there are the same conclusive reasons which are found in every cotton State in favor of manufacturing the cotton direct from the unpressed lint as it comes direct from the gin, but it will require time for these opportunities to be improved.

Mississippi, like the other States south of Virginia, was under the reckless rule that afflicted all and desolated many of the rebellious Commonwealths, but the Republican reign in this State was the best that has been known. Three Republicans filled the gubernatorial chair, and it is very generally admitted, even by their bitterest political foes, that none of them were personally corrupt. Governor Alcorn, the first Republican executive, is an old resident of the State, supported the Confederate cause after war had come, and is now a highly respected planter. He served only a short time as Governor, when he was elected to the Senate, from which body he retired to make a contest as a Conservative Republican against General Ames, who was then a Senator also. Alcorn was defeated by Ames, and he retired without stain upon his record either as Governor or Senator. Powers, the Lieutenant-Governor, succeeded Alcorn for two years. He gave a free rein to the profligacy that was necessary to keep the colored voters and their adventurous leaders together, but he is not accused of venality. He carpet-bagged from Ohio, but he continues to reside in the State, and is well respected. General Ames, son-in-law of General Butler, had an exceptional opportunity for a most brilliant and useful career for himself in Mississippi, but he failed disastrously. He was sent here as military governor, perfected reconstruction, was elected Senator for a full term when barely eligible in years, and a few years thereafter he left the Senate to become Governor by election over Senator Alcorn. He was not a politician, and he lacked the sagacity and tact necessary to the successful exercise of power. He ruled by military orders, and would not understand why he could not summarily depose a judge or make a law for himself in civil administration under a government of law, as he could under the military order of a despotic commander. He was impeached, and justly impeached, for gross disregard of law, but he realized the peril of his position before trial, and resigned to escape a dishonorable dismissal. It is due to him to say, however, that no charge of venality was preferred against him, and that his personal integrity stands practically unchallenged. It is remarkable to find three reconstruction Republican Governors in a negro State thus free from the stain of corruption, but Governors Alcorn, Powers, and Ames are fairly entitled to the creditable distinction. Political necessities made Powers and Ames assent to oppressive extravagance, as the newly enfranchised negro was first led out of the wilderness by leaders who appealed to his cupidity, passions, and love of indolence and luxury, but they were restrained from the destruction of State credit. They increased taxes for State purposes from three mills to fourteen mills, created some two millions of debt, and at one time had State and local taxes up to four per cent. in many localities; but the State took the easiest and cheapest way out from under the load by paying it dollar for dollar. Thus Mississippi, the only Southern State that had the imputation of repudiation against her before the war, is the only one that has emerged from reconstruction and carpet-bag rule without repudiating or adjusting a dollar of her carpet-bag debt. The State is now practically free from debt, excepting for a Chickasee school-fund of a million that cannot be paid, and her few bonds rate above par.

Mississippi is exceptionable also in the reputable character of her most prominent colored leaders. In all the other Southern States the negro leaders have rivalled the white adventurers in reckless and bewildering robbery, but they have not done so in Mississippi. Three black men have here reached national fame as leaders of their race, and they are all esteemed as honest men. Ex-Senator Revels was the first black man to enter the United States Senate, and in Washington, as in this State, he was respected by all who knew him as an intelligent and conscientious man. He is a minister, and has never brought reproach upon his sacred calling, even when prominent as a political leader. He did not have much love, however, for the sinuous ways of politics, and he retired to the presidency of a colored college, where he is enabled, by annual appropriations from the State, to educate his race in the higher branches of learning. His is one of three colored educational institutions in Mississippi. A normal school for colored teachers is maintained by the State, and the Baptists, with State aid, are successfully conducting a colored college. Senator Bruce is another of the noted negro leaders of the State, and he is respected by all. He became rich while sheriff and tax collector of Bolivar County, and he has been accused of corruptly securing his election to the Senate, but the charge of debauching the Legislature is not sustained. He cashed the depreciated State warrants of his impecunious colored brethren in the Senate and House at par, as he could so use the warrants in settling his accounts as collector, and his generous aid thus extended to his brethren without cost to himself made many resolve all doubts in his favor in the senatorial contest, but what he did was done in open day, and without discrimination in favor of his special friends. In short, he did just about what he likely would have done, more or less, for his race had there been no Senator to elect, and the charge of the corrupt control of his senatorial election is not warranted. He is uniformly spoken of with respect in Mississippi, and he could reside here, prosecute any business, and have more social sympathy from the better class of whites than he could command in Republican Philadelphia. He was born in slavery in this State, and educated himself as a Mississippi steamer cabin-boy. Like Revels, he has never sought to inflame the prejudices of race; his influence has been uniformly good, and he retired from the Senate without the blot of shame upon his skirts. Another black leader of note and power is Congressman Lynch, of Natchez. He was also born in slavery, and could not read or write when made free by general emancipation, but he possesses more than ordinary intelligence, and he speedily mastered the common rudiments of education. He was Speaker of the first Republican House, and he soon learned to preside with a degree of dignity and skill that has seldom been equalled by the cultivated whites who had made the position one of considerable honor, as was shown by the ability with which he presided over the Republican National Convention at Chicago in 1884. He has served in the Legislature and in Congress, and he has not been a corruptionist. He differs from most of his race in a taste for severe frugality rather than for improvidence, and he has accumulated a competence, but he cannot be justly accused of public dishonesty. These three men, admittedly the most able and prominent of the black leaders of Mississippi, have maintained the manhood that should be the pride of every race, and, much as Mississippi has suffered from the carpet-bag and colored rule, there has not been a tithe of the demoralization and waste here that has dishonored the reign of the black man in the Carolinas and the Gulf States. That much of this comparatively good record of a bad domination is due to Revels, Bruce, and Lynch, who successfully breasted the waves of corruption, is a fact that should be confessed and justly appreciated.

As Mississippi presents the most conspicuous cases of violent or fraudulent elections in the South, the subject may here be appropriately discussed. It is not pretended that there was any violent suppression or control of the negro vote in the late election in the South. The age of violence, as pictured in Judge Tourgee's "Fool's Errand," has passed away, and that book, while a faithful presentation of the South in the violent throes for the mastery of the destructive reign of the thief and adventurer, is now no more a true picture of the South than is "Uncle Tom's Cabin," in which the yoke of the bondman was so eloquently portrayed. The South had borne the merciless waste of the spoiler until the poverty of both races and the humiliation of the whites had made violence a comparative virtue. The Ku-Klux and the shot-gun did their work through the ignorant and brutal whites, who knew that their betters would deplore their acts but would not stay their hands. The law, that is as inexorable as the law of gravitation, asserted itself in the inevitable domination of superior intelligence and will. The hand of the thief was upon the throat of every property-owner, and public and private safety and social order imperatively demanded relief. The Federal government was voiced mainly or entirely through the jobbers, who made peace and the supremacy of law impossible, and insufferable wrongs righted themselves often by the worst of means. The question of the domination of race is now settled in the South, and it is settled beyond the power of national statutes or of official oppression or even of the gleaming bayonet to unsettle it. Both races understand it, and both are more content, more harmonious, and more prosperous to-day than at any time since the war closed.

This State has been discreditably notable for political tragedies for half a century. In old antebellum times, a Vicksburg or Natchez political editor who escaped a twelvemonth without a bullet or a Bowie-knife wound, was singularly fortunate. It is the State that bred the Bowies and gave

the world the Bowie-knife, and the bullet and the
blade have been much more the arbiters of party
disputes in the past than even in the turbulent times
since the war. The Prentisses and the Browns and
the Davises made the duel and the street-fight
respectable, and the ignorant accepted them with
the greater savagery that pertains to them. The
Chisholm and the Carrollton butcheries have their
score of counterparts in the past political contests
of Mississippi; but they were not then of national
moment. The killing of Chisholm and his daughter was unmixed and cowardly murder, for he was
a helpless prisoner and arraigned on what was a
false charge, although his murderers believed it to
be just. But even if he had been accessory to the
Gully murder, his butchery when alone, unarmed
and in prison, was the veriest mockery of courage
and murder without an extenuating circumstance.
It was in one of the proverbially lawless regions
of the State, where poverty, ignorance, and brutality
go hand in hand among both races, and there is
no more law for such crimes there than there was,
for more than ten years, in the murderous stronghold of the Mollie Maguires of Pennsylvania. The
Nixon tragedy of Yazoo was another of the regu-

lation Mississippi outcroppings of what has been
bred in the bone of the primitive settlers. Nixon
was an outlaw and a murderer, and he met the
doom he had more than once given to his foes;
but it was a crime, growing out of party dispute,
that the laws of any well-ordered community would
restrain by punishment, while in Yazoo punishment
is impossible. The Carrollton tragedy was the out-
cropping of brutalized race-hatred cherished by both
whites and blacks, in a few isolated sections. With
these tragedies the black race has had little to do,
nor were their rights involved in them; but, in
the sensitiveness of the North in regard to all
political tragedies in the South, they have done
much to cloud the name of Mississippi.

There is now great harmony between the races
in this State. Labor is abundant and well rewarded,
and the negroes are quite willing to take a respite
from the turmoil and demoralization of politics.
They tried it as a race, here as in the other Southern States, and they are not disposed to take the
field aggressively. They are gradually enlarging
their number of owners or lessees of cotton land,
and just as the negro gets enlisted in business he
ceases to care about politics, and least of all to

care about the more than doubtful rule of his race. Wealth is rapidly growing among both races in the State, and, while the advancement of Mississippi will be slower than most of the other Southern States, her people have everything to warrant their faith in a great future.

LOUISIANA.

LOUISIANA presents the most difficult shades of the great Southern problem that I have met with in all the varied aspects it offers in different communities. The question of race here is not entirely one of white and black. In part of New Orleans may be heard a modern Babel of tongues,—French, Spanish, German, Portuguese, with unintelligible English, and in the south and southwestern parishes the Latin race predominates among the whites. Louisiana stood alone among all the old States as rejecting the common for the civil law; the impress of the Latin blood is visible in both the Anglo-Saxon and the Ethiopian, and asserts itself visibly in the laws, in social regulations, and in the general policy of the Commonwealth. Sunday has always been the gala-day of the week, and the theatre, the ball, the old-time bull-fight, and all the devices of pleasure, are most worshipped on the day that the well-trained Anglo-Saxon holds as most sacred. The Latin blood is the old blood of Louisiana; it once reigned in unmixed purity and unvexed authority, and it has moulded the accretions from stranger blood much more than the Saxon will confess. I differ from most of the many intelligent citizens of the State I have met, in the belief that the widened diversity of races in Louisiana will prove an exceptional obstacle to the ultimate harmony of the white and black races in power and prosperity. The Latin blood that long reigned in the Crescent City and the rich plantations of the Gulf, answers to the pulsations of imperial tastes. It is not brutal; on the contrary, it is cultured and amiable, and it mingles more freely with the blood of the African than that of any other race, but it will rule the black man with less generous sympathy and co-operation for his advancement in citizenship than he receives even from the apostate Puritan.

Next to Virginia, Louisiana suffered more than any of the rebellious States during the war. New Orleans fell into the hands of the Union forces under General Butler when the Confederacy was in the zenith of its power and promise, and it was ruled with the iron heel that only war can wield. Her

commerce was cut off by the early possession of the
Upper Mississippi and by the siege of Vicksburg,
and thenceforth every issue of battle and every march
of contending armies added to her humiliation and
poverty; and when peace finally came, it found her
people scattered from their channels of industry, her
commerce destroyed, her wealth dissipated, and her
ignorant slaves the masters of her richest regions.
There was no such diversity of labor and ownership
in lands as prevailed in the border States and in the
grain belts of the Carolinas, Georgia, and Alabama.
Here all is in broad plantations, where sugar, rice,
and cotton are grown, and the small farmer was an
unknown factor in industrial progress. Under the
most favorable opportunities, the reorganization of
business and trade in the face of the violent changes
wrought by war, emancipation, and universal suffrage would have been one of the most difficult
problems of statesmanship; but when misrule and
the studied estrangement of races by appeals to ignorance, prejudice, and cupidity came as the first bitter
legacy of war, and waste was piled upon waste by the
long rule of the adventurer, reconstruction was indefinitely deferred in a tempest of demoralization.

Louisiana was ruled by the carpet-bagger and his

misguided ally, the black man, for ten long years, and no other State presents such appalling monuments of the desolation wrought by the adventurer. He found a people not only impoverished by the sudden loss of many millions of slave property, but also impoverished by the fearful waste of protracted war within her borders, and the possession of her chief centres by the Union army. Her plantations, the chief source of wealth, had been overrun or abandoned, and her marts of trade and wharves were guiltless of commerce. He found a legitimate debt of some eight millions and a State credit that had been scrupulously maintained until no government was left to reflect the integrity of the people. In this poverty and general desolation, the scourge of the carpet-bagger fell upon Louisiana, and the bitter cup of his creation had to be drunk to the dregs. In a single decade the positive debt of the State was increased to twenty-five millions, and the contingent or guaranteed debt to many millions more, making an aggregate of forty millions. Nor did he content himself with creating debt and wasting its proceeds. Reckless assessors were sent out among the people to value property for taxable purposes, and they were tempted to high valuations by being paid a percentage on the amount assessed; and upon these valuations the taxes for State purposes alone rose as high as twenty-one and a half mills. Trades, occupations, professions, and indeed everything that earned money, were also oppressively taxed, and with all this revenue and all the millions of increased debt, the interest, the schools, and the ordinary expenses of the government could not be met. The wealthy parishes were all dominated by the black vote, under the desperate leadership of the carpet-baggers, and, being without property themselves and inflamed against the whites, they imposed as high as two per cent. of parish taxes in some instances, which, with State and town and other local taxes, made from five to six per cent. the rate of taxation in many of the wealthiest portions of the Commonwealth. This terrible oppression came upon a people that had nothing but debt and devastated property, and the inevitable result was wide-spread bankruptcy, the depreciation of values from forty to sixty per cent., and a general paralysis of every channel of industry. Nor was the spoiler content with desolating the State. The city was rich in property and credit, and a legislative control of the municipal authority was assumed through legislative Park, School,

Police, Wharf, Levee, and other Commissions, by which New Orleans was practically bankrupted, and is staggering under a debt of twenty millions, with but little more than two hundred thousand population. The Wharf Commission crippled commerce by exorbitant fees on trade; the police were subordinated to partisan duties, and the schools were made a mockery of educational government. The legislative act authorizing the speculative pretence of draining the city at arbitrarily fixed prices from three to five times the legitimate cost of the work, and the legislative expenditure of ten millions for the State levees, during the ten years of carpet-bag rule, was lavished upon banded thieves by paying more than three times the prices now paid for the same work by the cubic yard.

Such a tide of bewildering profligacy could lead to but one end, and that was the utter destruction of credit and the inexorable call for a halt. Bonds had depreciated to nominal prices; interest could not be paid because the money was stolen by the ruling jobbers; the resources of the people from which money could be wrested had wellnigh perished, and the plunderer had to take pause, as there was no more plunder within his reach. State bonds had been recklessly issued by millions with little more than the color of law, and they had ceased to be marketable. In this utter despair of creditors, the Kellogg leaders, in 1874, decided to speculate on their own robberies, and they bought up, at nominal prices, the fraudulent bonds they had issued, and proposed to scale the whole debt, good, bad, and doubtful, at sixty cents on the dollar, in seven per cent. forty-year bonds. The old bona fide creditors of the State, who held the undisputed six per cent. bonds, were tempted to accept by the proffer of the reduced principal on increased interest, and the pools of fraudulent or doubtful bonds, held largely by the plunderers themselves at little or no cost, were promised protection against inquiry into their frauds and a fresh steal of many millions besides. They hastened to fund these bonds, and a constitutional amendment, declared as ratified by the election machinery common in Louisiana in those days, fastened a double fraud upon the people, first by a fraud upon the honest creditors, and next by a fraud that made millions of dishonest claims a constitutionally adjudicated debt of the State. When the Nichols government came into power in 1877, the disposition was very general to recog-

nize the scaled debt, regardless of the hardly disputed fraud that created nearly or quite half of it,
but two years of crop failures, added to the general
prostration of values and industry under ten years
of the most shameless robbery, made the burdens
of government oppressive, and it was not difficult
for the agitator to find willing hearers when he
demanded relief from fraudulent debt. Official reports made from all the parishes showed that the
reduction of values was fully one-half, and that by
the derangement of labor and successive unfavor-
able seasons for crops, the people were utterly un-
able to maintain the schools and the necessary expenses of the government and pay seven per cent.
interest on the funded debt. A Constitutional Convention was called, and before that body had reached
the question of the debt an amicable arrangement
had been practically agreed to by the creditors to
exchange their seven per cent. bonds for new four
per cents., which would have been an honest and
honorable solution of the question of State credit;
but repudiation had tasted blood in the exercise
of power, and an arbitrary settlement of the debt
was made by the convention fixing interest at two
per cent. for five years, three per cent. for fifteen

years, and four per cent. thereafter, with the right of creditors to fund immediately in a four per cent. bond at an abatement of twenty-five per cent. of the principal. This violent action of the convention, that embodied repudiation as one of its prominent attributes, was submitted to the people and ratified by a large majority. It would have been cheaper, much cheaper, to have borne the greater burdens for a few years and left their Commonwealth unspotted by the acceptance of the proffer of the creditors to receive four instead of seven per cent. interest. There can be but one judgment in regard to the arbitrary and indiscriminate reduction of interest, on a principal already indiscriminately scaled down forty per cent., and that must be an enduring stain upon the credit of the State. It will not be questioned that the extenuating circumstances have been fairly given herewith, but they fall far short of a reasonable excuse for what is ineffaceably stamped as actual repudiation.

There is the same general condition of the two races in Louisiana that is to be found in all the Southern States where the negro is numerically equal or stronger than the whites, with the exception that there is less sympathy for and inclination to political fellowship with the blacks among the old Latin blood than is common among the Anglo-Saxon. There is harmony between the races now because the professed friend of the negro impoverished him to starvation, and now the gradual revival of prosperity is greatly increasing his comfort. The utter and disgraceful failure of the rule that depended upon the colored race for its power has left the State, like most of the other Southern States, practically without a Republican organization, and the colored vote is not polled in most of the parishes. Where there has been an opportunity for a healthy organization of the party it has asserted itself without molestation, but most of the attempted reorganizations of the party have been by men who very naturally prostituted the Federal service to create violent disorder in their regions. There is less indication of division among the black voters here than in most of the other old Slave States, as few of them are property-owners and their business relations with the whites are not likely to become intimate here as elsewhere; but they understand that their Republican leaders left nothing but theft and misrule as the legacies of their power, and between their distrust of their leaders and the steady repressions by the whites, they feel no interest in politics. They know that they cannot rule, and they know that, as they are now situated, they should not rule. A political campaign means grinding the black man between the upper and the nether millstone of thieving friends and brutal foes, and until there shall be a Republican organization in Louisiana that merits some measure of trust from both whites and blacks, the strength of the colored vote will be unfelt in elections. The State is very slowly recovering her prosperity, but it will be the work of years to make the general thrift and comfort of either race that prevailed before the war.

In 1785 eight bales of cotton were shipped to Europe. It was the first consignment of cotton from the New World to the Old, and it dated the advent of a commerce that has grown to hundreds of millions annually, and that reaches every industrial centre of Europe. It is now one of the most important factors in clothing the world, and it gives employment to many millions of people in every progressive civilization. From the day that the field-hand plants the seed until it fulfils its multiplied missions, from clothing both culture and barbarism until it ends in the pages of the Bible in the heathen land or in the newspaper that reaches every American home, cotton is ever increasing industry, commerce, and thrift, and magnifying wealth and comfort; and it was the centennial anniversary of the birth of this important product that inspired the New Orleans Exposition. Only a few years ago the South joined the peoples of the earth in celebrating the centennial anniversary of the immortal Declaration of Independence, and now the North is joining the South and the nations of Europe, of the far South and of the western shore of the Pacific, in celebrating the birth of cotton commerce. And it is fitly done in New Orleans, the great commercial centre acquired for the then infant Republic by Jefferson, the author of the matchless chart of freedom that has created the noblest government of man. By the purchase of Louisiana from France, Jefferson's far-reaching sagacity and statesmanship secured the source and the outlet of the Father of Waters, that now gathers commerce from twenty-eight States and Territories of the Union for this great mart of trade.

The Exposition was a financial failure, but it accomplished great good to the nation. The government was compelled to come to the rescue of the original Cotton Exposition of last year to save it from financial collapse, but that did not deter the active business element of New Orleans from embarking in a new Exposition to continue the present season. The pluck, energy, and sacrifice necessary to rehabilitate the Exposition were found in the Crescent City and the South, and the reorganization of the enterprise on the ruins of failure with liberal government aid, proves that Southern people understand the new order of things, and are hastening Southern development by wise and tireless effort. The opening of new channels of trade with Mexico and Central and South America by the Exposition far surpassed the most sanguine expectations of New Orleans, and the reorganized Exposition doubtless owes its existence to the growing trade with these countries. The Northern States have greatly undervalued or practically overlooked the great lesson of the New Orleans Exposition. It is, in fact, the gateway for a new, large, and profitable trade with the tropical countries south of us, and had there been the cordial and general co-operation with New Orleans that the Exposition well deserved, the benefits of our enlarged trade with the South American countries would be almost incalculable. As it is, with both Expositions financial failures, their beneficial results will be felt in the future as we sluggishly gather up the trade that could and should have been stimulated into immediate activity by all sections of the country utilizing the proffered advantages of the Exposition.

There is one withering blight that spreads its baleful shadows upon the State of Louisiana, and that is the Louisiana Lottery Company. That it is only legalized robbery of the people here and elsewhere, or illegal robbery under color of law, is evident to all who learn from its own confession in official publications, that it returns to policy patrons little more than half the money it gathers from them; but when its social, political, and business demoralization is considered; its systematic robbery of the best attributes of communities; of the qualities of legitimate industry and of the business integrity that alone can make a respected and prosperous people, it is as "the pestilence that walketh in darkness and the destruction that wasteth at noonday." This corporation, whose trade was recently declared by the Philadelphia United States Court to be "an infamous crime," muzzles the press of the South, ramifies its power into political, social, and judicial circles, and multiplies the poverty of war among the people. It is lavish in its gifts, ostentatious in its charities, and generous in public enterprise, but the Church could as well draw its financial sustenance from the bawdy-house or the gambler's den, and hope to promote vital piety, as can the politics, charity, or enterprise of New Orleans draw tribute with self-respect from the lottery swindle.

NASHVILLE—TENNESSEE.

Of the old cities of the South, Nashville ranks next to Atlanta in rapid and substantial growth since the war. It has many signs of Northern energy and thrift, and it is advancing with healthy strides. Standing at the Capitol, where a grand panoramic view is presented of the undulating hills which surround the city, it looks like home to one who loves the mountains and valleys of Pennsylvania. The city proper stands on an elevation that centres in an almost circular valley, through which the Cumberland passes, washing the skirts of the forest-clad hills around it: and handsome residences, colleges, and monuments of beneficent effort dot the elevated plateaus. From one view of the Capitol portico you see the Fisk University, where more than three hundred colored students, embracing both sexes, are being fitted as teachers of their race. Another view presents the Vanderbilt University, the one col-

136

lege of the land that records a munificent charity by the elder Vanderbilt. The Baptist College near by adds its testimony to the imposing temples of the Fisk University, in teaching the North how the South outstrips the antislavery States in the education of the black man. On nearly every side may be seen the dark, heavy columns of smoke that point out the many hives of industry the city can boast of. The frowns of winter, which make the highways snow-bound or ice-bound in Pennsylvania, are tempered, as a rule, to gentle frosts and flitting snows in this latitude, and winter seems only to nestle in the lap of spring. There is no more beautiful city south of the Ohio than the capital of Tennessee. Its almost exceptional natural advantages and attractions have been well appreciated and developed by its enterprising and hospitable people, and but for the sable faces which divide the multitude in many sections of the city, the sojourner could not distinguish it as of the South. The exquisite equestrian statue of Jackson stands close to the Capitol building, where the morning sunlight can make the dews glitter as jewels in the chaplets of the more than venerated chieftain, and the people of Tennessee must forget the devotion of their fathers before another statue can divide the honor of a place in the beautiful Capitol grounds.

When the war began, Tennessee owed some twenty millions, of which about sixteen millions were for railroads which were solvent and paid their interest, leaving about four millions as the actual debt of the State. But reconstruction brought to Tennessee, as it did to the other rebellious States, an utterly reckless and profligate State rule. The erratic and desperate Brownlow made himself Governor by Union bayonets, had a general legislative ticket voted for where polls could be opened, and thus made up a Legislature composed of some honest Union men, some skulkers from both armies, and an assortment of negroes. Some of them were declared elected from counties in which they did not receive a single vote, and where there was no pretence of an election; but Brownlow wanted a government and he thus made it. In 1869, after two years of Brownlow's highly original illustration of popular government, he was re-elected, as he disfranchised all who had ever aided rebellion and appointed his own election officers. He then elected himself to the Senate, leaving Dewitt C. Senter, the Lieutenant-Governor, in the executive chair. Governor Senter saw that

Brownlow rule could not last, as it had given birth to the Ku-Klux and general insecurity to both person and property, and he began to conserve Republican authority. He was denounced by Brownlow and his reckless followers for his hesitation, and they nominated General Stokes to succeed him; but Senter had learned Brownlow's ways of carrying elections, and he took the field against Stokes, appointed his own election officers, and made a regulation Brownlow majority against the Brownlow party. Thus the rule of the adventurer was overthrown in 1870; but meantime the Brownlow administration had increased the debt nearly thirty millions, making an aggregate of nearly fifty millions, with less than three hundred millions of taxable property in the entire State. The taxes were largely increased and the available resources of the State were expended, leaving Tennessee with a mountain of debt and generally impoverished. In 1873 the first practical effort was made to adjust the debt. The Brownlow government, after more than doubling the debt with little compensation to the State, by the issue of bonds to speculative railroad combinations, passed a law authorizing railway companies to pay their debt to the State in any of the State bonds. Some of the bonds were worth only nominal rates in market, and the solvent railways, whose bonds made up a considerable portion of the old debt, bought up the worthless bonds floating on the market and liquidated their accounts with the State. By this process and the selling out at almost total loss of the railroads invented by plunderers, the actual debt was reduced to twenty-one millions, instead of about four millions before the war, and that debt was funded at six per cent. and the interest paid for one year. In 1874 an additional debt of two millions was precipitated upon the State for immediate payment, by the Supreme Court of the United States making the State liable for that amount of the notes of the Bank of Tennessee. The notes were receivable for taxes, thus reducing the revenues two millions in one year, and that was the feather that broke the camel's back. That was the end of the maintenance of credit in Tennessee, and the gate once opened, the flood increased with each year, until all debt-payers were swept from power, and creditors were finally compelled to choose between a reduction of fifty per cent. of profit with three per cent. interest or general repudiation. With all classes and interests impoverished by war, with debt tainted by the creative touch

of the adventurer, and politicians ready to appeal to
the cupidity and necessities of the people, it is not
surprising that when the current of repudiation is
once started, it speedily swells to a flood-tide.

Tennessee, like Alabama, has been greatly blessed
in her natural gifts to invite every diversity of legitimate industry, and the hopeful promise of her future
is in the very general interest exhibited by all classes
of business men to promote the development of her
vast wealth. Instead of discussing politics or wrang-
ling over offices, the one question most earnestly discussed in public places, in the clubs, and in social
gatherings that draw the men of substance, is the
best method of attracting industrial emigrants, of
securing capital and business experience to multiply
producing mines, furnaces, factories, farms, railways,
and schools. An evening spent as profitably as
pleasantly at one of the clubs of the city, discussed only the question of how to make the
stranger most welcome as a citizen of the State.
The young business men of Nashville were at the
front, and with them were the college professor,
the journalist, the minister, and the politician of
the New South. They have buried the past and
its dead; they have buried with it the traditions,

the teachings, the prejudices which made the South
the home of a few in luxury and the home of
many in poverty. They discuss slavery only as one
of the sad errors of their fathers, and they welcome
emancipation as the disenthralment of the whites
quite as much as the disenthralment of the blacks.
They are, as a class, the men who learned in boy-
hood, by the terrible sacrifices of war, that "hardness ever of hardiness is mother," and they have
grown to manhood since the story of Appomattox
was dated. They have grown up self-reliant and
energetic, and they are about to assert themselves
in the political and business policy of the whole
South. Even South Carolina has a Governor who
won his position as the founder of the liberal educational system of the Palmetto State and not as
a Confederate warrior, and the sudden and irresistible impetus about to be given to the material development of the South will speedily subordinate
the heroes and memories of the war to the better
achievements of peaceful progress. This element
demands the prompt development of the diversified
wealth of Tennessee; the early completion of her
great water-ways; the opening of her iron, coal,
copper, and marble deposits; the employment of

her immense water-powers to whirl the spindle and drive the loom and forge-hammer, and they want just protection for the industries of the nation. More than that, they will have what they need if united and manly effort can attain it, regardless of partisan leaders or free-trade dreamers.

No intelligent business man from Pennsylvania can carefully examine the natural resources of Tennessee and Alabama without seeing the hand of destiny that is soon to mark a revolution in the iron and coal trade of this country. While in the single struggle for the mastery in iron and coal product, Alabama has in some measure the advantage of Tennessee as a great centre of those commodities, this State surpasses Alabama in the surroundings of mineral wealth, which can be profitably developed by manufacturing. The soil of Tennessee is better than that of Pennsylvania, and capable of every growth we can boast of in the Keystone State, with cotton added in a large belt of the southern portion. It has all the diversity of hills, valleys, and water-courses, with a more congenial climate. East Tennessee has as just claim to be called the Switzerland of America as has Northern Pennsylvania. In addition to fourteen thousand

square miles of productive lands and half a million
population, it has one hundred and fifty miles of
navigable waters leading to the great commercial
centres of the South. Middle Tennessee, although
an inland country, with nearly a million people,
has five hundred miles of navigable waters; has four
thousand square miles containing iron ore, and was
an iron-producing region before the war of 1812.
West Tennessee borders on the Father of Waters,
that will evermore, I trust, "go unvexed to the
sea," and these natural highways are certain to
hasten the mastery of the South in mineral products which have hitherto been most successfully
produced in the North. I have in a previous chapter
explained how the opening of the Warrior River,
at a cost of less than is annually wasted on the
River and Harbor bill on mud creeks, would open
the great Alabama coal- and iron-fields to the world.
It was urged by John Quincy Adams when President, but diversified industry and slavery were foes,
and the more importunate North and West took
the appropriations. In like manner the great iron-
and coal-fields of Tennessee have been shut out
from the markets of the world by the mussel shoals
in the Tennessee River, although Tennessee has

had Jackson, Polk, and Johnson as Presidents, and could and should have had an uninterrupted water-way to the Gulf half a century ago. But neces-sity is an impressive teacher, and now Tennessee will successfully demand the improvement of her obstructed natural highway. Then her iron and coal, more abundant and more easy of access than the iron and coal of Pennsylvania, will enter every competing centre, and her marble, more than ample to rebuild the Appian Way of Rome, as Balie Peyton elegantly expressed it at our Philadelphia Centennial, will enrich the architecture of every civilization. These improvements are near at hand, and they will date the successful rivalry of the South in the great mineral products of Pennsyl-vania.

The iron trade in Tennessee is no new enter-prise. As early as 1810 charcoal iron was pro-duced in Middle Tennessee, and there were thirty-five charcoal-furnaces in successful operation here in 1860. A full half-century ago, in 1832 I believe, the Philadelphia Franklin Institute made a series of tests of the various qualities of iron in the American markets, and declared the iron of Tennessee equal to the Swedish iron in ductility and firmness of texture; and it is one of the traditions of the State that no Mississippi River steamboat boiler made of Tennessee iron was ever exploded. In both coal and iron it is evident that we have no advantage in quality in Pennsylvania over Tennessee, except as we employ foreign ores to improve our native product; but as water navigation to the very heart of the iron- and coal-fields of Alabama and Tennessee will offer cheaper facilities for the mixture of foreign ores with the native ores of the South, the advantages of quality we now possess are not enduring. Tennessee has over five thousand square miles of the great Appalachian coal-field of the continent; it has four thousand square miles containing rich red and brown hematite ores, and, like Alabama, it has the iron, coal, and limestone in close proximity. The highest estimate I have had from experienced iron men as the average cost of producing iron in this State is eleven dollars and fifty cents per ton, and many claim that every well-appointed and managed furnace produces it as low as ten dollars and sixty cents. Birmingham now ships iron to Philadelphia, Pittsburg, and New England, as I saw by the books of leading furnace men there; but Birmingham and Tennessee now control the iron markets of the large iron-consuming States of Indiana and Illinois. Birmingham can ship to Philadelphia or New York by rail to Charleston or Savannah, and thence by water, for three dollars and eighty cents per ton; it can reach Indianapolis for three dollars and seventy-five cents, and Tennessee can reach the West for a little less. These are the rates with the present necessarily expensive transportation; and what will be increased advantage of Tennessee and Alabama in coal and iron, when multiplied capital and riper experience and largely increased product shall cheapen both the product and its transportation? These facts present a grave problem to the great coal and iron industries of the North, and they must and will be squarely and intelligently looked in the face. I do not fear that the South will destroy the coal and iron industries of Pennsylvania, for that is impossible; but I am convinced that it will speedily revolutionize both. Business follows natural laws as surely as the stars follow their appointed courses in the heavens, and I look for the North to hasten the transfer of much of its capital and business experience to the virgin and more inviting coal- and iron-fields of Tennessee and Alabama. It will be done because the obstacles of slavery, of civil war, and of lingering distrust, which have hitherto been insuperable, are about to perish, and North and South will be bound together by the indissoluble ties of business interest.

FLORIDA—ORANGE-GROWING.

THE Goddess of Romance illumines the history of Florida. It was the earliest of all the discoveries on the Western continent; was explored from the mouth of the St. John to the Father of Waters by De Soto nearly three and a half centuries ago, and he was only the follower of Ponce de Leon, who had taken possession of it in 1512 in the name of the Spanish king and named it the Land of Flowers. Before the Revolutionary war with Britain, the warriors of England and Spain had two centuries of battle for the possession of Florida, that was ended by Spain ceding the territory to the United States nearly seventy years ago. Soon after our acquisition of the long-disputed country a bloody Indian war followed, lasting nearly a decade, until Osceola, the famed Seminole warrior chief, pined his restless life away as a prisoner in Charleston. Hard by historic Fort Moultrie the savage warrior sleeps, conquered only

by death, and shattered remnants of his once proud
and heroic tribe now wander through the Everglades,
guiltless of war-paint and battle-axe. It is a strange
story that this first discovered, explored, and settled
portion of the continent was comparatively an unknown country for three hundred years after its dis-
covery, and when Florida was admitted as a State
half a century ago, it was as a political necessity to
strengthen the South in the Senate, rather than as
an aid to the development of a new Commonwealth.
Little progress was made in Florida until after the
late civil war, when its genial climate, its bountiful
orchards and gardens, its perennial verdure and flowers, its grand forests, its romantic rivers, its more
than a thousand miles of sea-coast, and its restful
and recuperating winter resorts for invalids, began to
attract Northern visitors to this lovely winter garden
of the Union. The St. John's River is one of the
great natural water highways of the country. Unlike
all others, it flows from the far Southern coast north-
ward, and while its whole line is not over four hundred miles, its tributaries give it a thousand miles of
navigation. Its upper waters present a series of navigable lakes some of which are several miles in
breadth, and it closely hugs the ocean in its whole

course as it comes to greet the waters of the North, with its banks luxuriant in tropical growth. The quaint old city of St. Augustine, below the mouth of the great river, is rich in legend and romance. More than half a century before the tread of the Pilgrims on Plymouth Rock, Menendez had founded his colony there, and built up a fortified city only to be pillaged and destroyed by Drake, the British freebooter, as Menendez had exterminated the Huguenots south of the St. John's by flame and sword a few years before; but the Spaniard rebuilt his city and Fort San Marco, that resisted every assault in the conflicts of Spain and England, even when the city was captured. Its historic City Gate, with its antique towers, is the lingering relic of the old wall that crossed the little peninsula to defend the often assailed first city of North America.

The people of the North know Florida chiefly as the land of oranges, and there is a flavor of romance about orange-growing that captivates the plodding husbandman and entices the fancy farmer. It seems to be such a delectable occupation, where little labor among perennial verdure and fragrant blossoms is supposed to produce a bountiful harvest of doubly golden fruit, and thousands have plunged headlong

into it, both as small farmers ready to do their own
work, and as speculative or fancy tillers of the
Florida soil, while comparatively few have realized
their expectations of profit and many have given up
in despair or bankruptcy. These experiences are in
no degree the fault of the orange-growing industry,
but they are precisely the experiences that Southern
orange-growers or cotton-planters would meet if they
attempted Pennsylvania or Western farming with
their limited knowledge of the methods by which
Northern agriculture is made profitable. Orange-
growing is just like the growing of wheat, corn, potatoes, oats, cotton, rice, or tobacco; it must be understood, and understood in the most practical way, to
make it pay; and that understanding must apply
as well to the selection of the particular soil and
climate of Florida as to the planting, rearing, till-
ing, fertilizing, and generally caring for the orchards
which are expected to bring fortune to the owner.
Orange-orchards thus selected or planted and thus
handled with the intelligence and fidelity they need
are among not only the most profitable, but also
among the most certain crops grown on the continent. I present this statement with the full knowledge, gained largely by personal investigation, that

more than half the entire orange crop of this year has been destroyed. The loss of the orange-growers this winter is not less than one million dollars from the destructive winter, and the loss of early vegetables is from half a million to a million more; but this large loss to dishearten the Florida orange- and vegetable-growers, has led to exhaustive inquiry into the comparative losses of staple crops in all sections of the country, and it clearly proves that there is no State in the Union where crops are more certain or more profitable than in Florida, and of these, the more delicate products, which have suffered so severely this winter, are among the most certain and profitable of all. When it is remembered that the destructive frost of this winter in Florida has not been known since 1835, or for more than half a century, and that there is not a staple crop of the North that is not half destroyed once in five years by some of the many causes which reduce or kill the growing crops of Northern fields, the intelligent reader will understand the logic of my conclusions.

Hap-hazard orange-growing is just like hap-hazard wheat- or corn-growing. Sometimes it will happen to pay; but generally it will not pay, and the disappointed farmer is usually ready to blame everything

but himself when he alone is in fault.   There is no
more inviting State than Florida for the laboring
man who aims to acquire a small farm and do his
own work, as do most Western settlers.   A small
orange grove well located, well planted, well tilled,
and well cared for, all of which are within the
capacity of the owner himself, is certainly the easiest
and surest way to increase the value of both plant
and product.   It will require five to eight years
before profitable crops of oranges can be gathered,
but good orange land is capable of producing all
the necessaries of life, except wheat, with less labor
than even on the prairies of the West.   Beef and
pork can be raised with little cost beyond the original investment, and the fact that they can be raised
so easily, seems to forbid the little effort and care
needed to raise them well.   The small farmer has
everything to invite him to Florida, but he is of a
class that is most liable to be deceived and robbed
by the land speculators who are thick as flies where
there are opportunities for plying their vocation.
There are millions of acres of land in Florida,
which are valueless, at least for the present generation, and of the many millions which are really
valuable, wise discrimination is necessary in select-

ing lands for orange and vegetable culture. In the Indian River region, it would be easy for any one of ordinary intelligence to select profitable lands, but those lands now cost as much per acre as do the model farms of Lancaster County. It has been the home of the most luscious orange of the world for years, and it is there that strawberries are grown in perfection in open air in mid-winter and command two dollars a quart in the Northern cities. It is simply perpetual summer, and the tropical fruits are grown there in profusion; but the small farmer, seeking a home to be built up by his own patient labor, can't afford to purchase Indian River farms, and he must go into some of the other promising sections of the State. Fortunately, they are abundant. They don't offer the climate and products of the Indian River region, but they offer probably as great results from the same investment. It is in the selection of land in Florida that the first danger to the immigrant is presented. As a rule he has neither the means nor the knowledge of the State necessary to select just what he needs, and he can buy apparently good land, give it the labor and the care that should give him good returns, and yet fail in his undertaking. The soil is more variable than the climate. Some portions possess the proper qualities and surroundings to produce good orange crops with the minimum amount of outlay and labor, and others, apparently equally inviting, will require costly fertilizing or irrigation, or both, to produce abundant crops. Farms of from twenty to forty acres are large enough for successful small farming, and small farming is the most substantial and profitable enterprise in the growth of a State. The mere speculator comes and goes and seldom benefits either land or people; but the small farmer comes to stay; to multiply wealth; to found communities, commerce, railways, newspapers, schools, and churches, and he is the greatest source of both public and private wealth. When he fails, the State feels it, for failure in the community chills the pulsations of the heart of the Commonwealth.

I could not instruct any person how to grow the orange successfully, as I am quite as ignorant of the tree and its needs as are nine-tenths who attempt to grow it and fail; but I have learned enough to know how much the orange-grower must learn before he can depend upon his orange-orchards for profit. While there is absolutely greater certainty of crops and of profit in orange farming in Florida than in any farming in the North, the orange-tree is a coy and wayward growth, and needs intelligent and affectionate caressing. It is neither difficult to manage nor abstruse in the theories which make it an appreciative and profitable pet; but its soil and its wants must be understood, and its wants must be supplied; but even the labor and expenditure necessary to bring it to the highest perfection should be profitable. The best possible culture of the infant orange-orchard is the growth of vegetables, etc., from the soil while the trees are pushing forward to the bearing period; and thus, while the farmer is giving his orange-trees the cultivation and fertilizers they need, he can be gathering his three crops a year of the necessaries of life. Instead of waiting a year for results, as must the small farmer of the West, and be brought to the verge of starvation by a single fatal visitation of untimely frost or of the cyclone or the grasshopper, he can begin any season of the year and have his corn and vegetables on his table in three months, and be giving to his orange-trees the attention they so scrupulously demand. But the orange is as bountiful in variety as is the apple, and soil, climate, and variety of fruit must be in harmony, or the results will be unsatisfactory. The same is true of most crops of the field in the North and West; but the fruits and vegetables of Florida are much more delicate than the staple crops of the Northern farmer, and adaptability of variety of crop to particular soil and climate is imperative here, while it is only a question of degree of success or failure in the North. The State presents the distinct features of semi-tropical, sub-tropical, and tropical climate. From Jacksonville southward there is a more and more sunny clime until the keys south of Biscayne Bay are absolutely frostless, but they, with the sub-tropical region still dominated by the fragments of the Seminole, are not yet inhabited by settlers. The medium between the semi-tropical and the tropical is commonly spoken of as beyond the frost-line, but it is a fiction, of course, although frost is seldom serious and never destructive of entire crops of oranges and vegetables, as was common in the northern section this year. With new settlements now rapidly extending southward, and with railways rapidly following the lines of improvement, the settler can get beyond serious peril from frost, and can, in most instances, protect his crops. Thus climate, soil, and variety of fruit all enter into successful orange-growing, and almost every variety of semi-tropical climate and soil are now open to the settler at lower rates than land equally accessible to markets can be obtained anywhere in the West.

Very few people in the North have any intelligent conception of the orange industry of Florida. It is less than a quarter of a century since the Florida orange became an important article of commerce, and it is now much less than one-tenth the product of the orange-orchard consumed in the United States. Florida harvested eighty millions of oranges in 1885, and would have harvested more than that number this year but for the destructive winter, while we import seven hundred millions annually, chiefly from Sicily. California grows a large orange crop, but the cost of transportation has hindered it from reaching the market east of the great mountains. Here is the great orange-field of the continent; the orchards which produce the finest fruit of the world, and the future of the Florida orange product almost defies calculation. Fully two-thirds of the orange-orchards of the State are under ten years of age, and half that number, or one-third of the whole, are not five years old. Most of the old and bearing orchards have been grown carelessly, and their product is lessened both in quantity and quality by the failure to appreciate the necessity of growing the best trees in the best soil and in the best manner; but the orchards now beginning to bear, and the younger ones, have, as a rule, been located, planted, and nurtured with intelligent care, and they, and the rapidly-multiplying orchards of the early future, must revolutionize the orange trade within another score of years, and exclude the less-inviting foreign fruit from our markets. Neither the oldest inhabitants nor even tradition can fix the period when the orange-tree gives up its work. It will bear in from six to twelve years from the seed, or two years earlier from the average nursery twig, according to climate. The Kissimmee tree will bear three years earlier than the Jacksonville tree, and as the orange cultivation extends southward, the tree hastens the bearing period. The first crop from a tree in fair bearing condition will be about two hundred, and with proper care its crop will increase from twenty to forty per cent. for twenty or thirty years. There are trees in the State which bear ten thousand oranges yearly, and many which bear five thousand, but they are exceptional, of course. It needs only a little use of simple arithmetic to prove that the orange crop of Florida must reach ten millions of dollars annually in a few years, instead of the present product of two millions, and as the orange product increases all other products must steadily increase, although in a less ratio of value, and the rapidly-increasing facilities for transportation, and the accepted superiority of the Florida fruit, must ever maintain profitable markets for this now important and swiftly-increasing product.

I have specially discussed the question of orange-growing from the stand-point of the small farmer, as that is the class that Florida most needs, and it is the class that most needs Florida. The same general laws which govern successful orange-growing for small farmers govern the industry in all its phases; but the capitalist who mingles pleasure and healthful winter enjoyment with profit, is generally able to select his location and invest wisely. There are a number of such orange plantations on the St. John's, which pay largely on the investment, besides furnishing beautiful and healthful winter homes for their owners, and the whole line of the railway from Sanford south to Kissimmee City is beautified by attractive winter homes with orange-orchards either beginning to bear or giving promise of early and bountiful crops. Just as settlements and railways extend southward will the orange-orchards extend with them, and better fruit and surer profits will be attained. The Florida orange industry is indeed a wonderful development, although yet in its infancy, and the present generation will see it the first in value of the products of the State, instead of falling behind cotton, lumber, and corn, as it does now.

FLORIDA—HEALTH AND PRODUCTS.

STARTLING as is the transformation of Florida in many other sections of the State, in St. Augustine, the oldest city of the continent, that lay dormant for nearly three centuries, the march of improvement as a popular winter resort is obviously taking the lead. Two years ago it was deemed a doubtful enterprise to build the San Marco House, capable of giving first-class entertainment to three or four hundred guests, but it is now about to be obscured by the Ponce de Leon, to cost a million dollars for the structure alone, with probably half as much more to furnish and beautify, and it is not doubted that its thousand guests will be ready for it as soon as it can be opened next season. There are a full score of large hotels in the State which equal or surpass the best class of summer resort hotels in the North in all the essential qualities of comfort, and the smaller hotels and boarding-houses

163

of various grades which are sought by invalids in search of quiet and rest and by visitors of moderate means are reckoned by the hundreds. Not only in Jacksonville and St. Augustine are the hotels of the very best class in all respects, but elegant hotels abound at Palatka, Sanford, Enterprise, Winter Garden, Orlanda, Kissimmee, and many other places on the St. John's River and on the new lines of railroad. The hotels throughout Florida within range of Northern visitors are vastly better than the hotels of the prominent inland cities of Pennsylvania or New York or New England, and in the chief centres they rival the more pretentious hotels of Philadelphia and New York in the excellence of their table and the comfort of their rooms. But even these hotels, which were deemed extravagant ventures only a few years ago, will now be eclipsed by the Ponce de Leon of St. Augustine, which will be comparable only with the hotel palaces of the Pacific coast in colossal proportions, grandeur, and completeness in all appointments; and what shall now be done in St. Augustine will be speedily imitated, only on a lesser scale of expenditure, in the localities which are rapidly developing as permanent centres of Northern visitors. I hazard little in saying that the present generation will see scores of hotels in Florida far outstripping the most popular and costly watering-places of the North alike in number and elegance. There is only one Florida in North America. It was until lately far distant from the North, but now swift express trains with almost every comfort of home, and rapid coast steamers from every Northern commercial port, have brought the "Land of Flowers" within easy reach of pleasure-seekers and invalids; and the prospect of profitable investments has turned a steadily growing tide of all classes of money-getters to Florida, from the conservative capitalist to the head-long speculator. These lessons of the future of the State are clearly visible to the intelligent observer even in the severest winter desolation that Florida has known for half a century, and each year will vindicate the view I present with surprising and substantial certainty.

While the tide of invalids from the North to the softer winter climate of Florida is rapidly multiplying, there is a popular apprehension that miasma prevails in the State and that malarial fevers are likely to greet the settler in many sections. It is the natural assumption of those who are not fully

informed on the subject, that a new country abound-
ing in lakes, lagoons, and other bodies of water
overflowing their channels or without apparent
channels of outlet, must breed malaria; but in
point of fact, as proved alike by reason and well-
tested experience, there is less malaria in Florida
than in Pennsylvania; much less than in the new
Western States or in the other coast States of the
South. Two-thirds of the State is a peninsula across
which sweep the healthy breezes from Gulf to
Ocean, and there are no mountains to impede their
progress. The highest altitude does not reach five
hundred feet above tide, and no part of Florida,
except the extreme northern line, is ever free from
the flavor of the sea. This fact considered in connection with the general absence of stagnant waters,
dispels the theory of a malarial atmosphere. Instead
of the stagnant and putrid waters of the North and
West, Florida has countless subterranean currents of
the fresh waters from the Appalachian range, which
furnish flowing wells of pure water by driving down
through soft earth from three to five hundred feet,
and these underground lakes feed and drain most
of the lake regions of the State. Jacksonville has
an ample supply of water from several flowing wells

just on the edge of the city, none of which is four hundred feet in depth. Of course, there is malaria in Florida if the visitor is foolish enough to hunt for it. There are marshes here as elsewhere; the rapid flow of immigration and the sudden cultivation of hundreds of thousands of acres; the false economy that accepts surface water for drinking when wholesome water can be obtained anywhere much cheaper from wells than in Pennsylvania, and the indolence that invites the disorders of the Florida limestone water in the sections where that soil prevails, must produce light fevers here as they would produce graver disease in the North; but there is no new State in which sickness is less common than it is in Florida, and there is no other State in which the diseases peculiar to the region can be so easily and so effectually guarded against. One of the most prolific sources of ill health among settlers from the colder climate of the North is the unwillingness to learn that the strong diet necessary there is not only not needed here, but is the source of many physical disorders. The Pennsylvania mountaineer can thrive on his pork, sausage, and buckwheat cakes swimming in grease, but when he seeks the climate of Florida, he must obey the law of nature that adapts the growth of the climate to the needs and comfort of the husbandman. Surgeon-General Lawton justly declared that " Florida possesses a much more agreeable and salubrious climate than any other State or Territory in the Union," and he answered the question of the alleged malarial nature of the atmosphere by official statistics, showing that while in the Middle division of the United States the percentage of deaths from remittent fever is one in thirty-six; in the Northern division one in fifty-two; in the Southern division one in fifty-four; in Texas one in seventy-eight; and in California one in one hundred and forty-eight, in Florida it is only one in two hundred and eighty-seven. Considering that the summers in Florida are long and often severely trying, with the natural causes which would produce epidemics in the North in the absence of complete drainage and wholesome water, it is no less marvellous than true that the general healthfulness of Florida surpasses that of any other State in the Union. Judging from the causes which would be productive of fevers and general ill-health in the North, malaria and the many disorders which attend it would naturally be expected in the large portion of Florida just reclaimed from water by the great Disston enterprise. I saw a thriving little city at Kissimmee where the present streets were passable only in boats three years ago, and around it thousands of acres rescued from the bottom of the lakes and much of it now under cultivation; but fevers are almost unknown, and the first case of sunstroke, pneumonia, diphtheria, smallpox, or yellow fever has yet to occur. The laboring force employed by the Philadelphia Draining Company is composed entirely of white men, many of whom are from the North, and the last official report of Chief Engineer James M. Kreamer, well known in Philadelphia, makes the remarkable statement that in all their operations since 1881, "there has never been a death from any cause, and a physician in a professional capacity has never visited our work." The drainage, exposure, and cultivation of such an area on the Susquehanna, Juniata, or Delaware Rivers, would depopulate the region by deadly malaria.

The more I have seen of and inquired into the general product of labor in Florida, the more I am impressed with the advantages this State presents to actual settlers over the far West, and even over all the other Southern States. When I first publicly

15*

suggested, five years ago, that the day is not distant
when the tide of surplus labor, from both our own
and foreign lands, must turn from the West to the
South, there were few who credited it, while many
vigorously combated it. Even intelligent men in the
South, fully appreciating the need of actual settlers
and earnestly desiring to encourage them, gave little
credence to the prediction, while both North and
West generally resented it ; but what was discredited
prophecy then is rapidly shaping into history now.
The surplus young men from our Pennsylvania farms
have not yet turned Southward in any considerable
numbers, but their forerunners are now rearing cotton-mills, furnaces, machine-shops, and railways in
the reconstructed States, and the farmer will follow as
surely as day succeeds the night. The next decade
will see scores of thousands of our surplus skilled
laborers settled in the South ; capital will bring them
to the more inviting and certain fields of investment,
and the tide of both home and foreign immigration
that seeks lands for homes, will soon learn to prefer
the cheaper lands of the South with better markets
and the best possible product of a given amount of
labor. The wheat-, corn-, and stock-growers have a
vast domain open to them in the Virginias, the Caro-

linas, Tennessee, Georgia, and Alabama, which have their tobacco, cotton, and rice belts, with boundless mineral wealth, and Florida adds to cotton, corn, rye, oats, and lumber her matchless fruits and vegetables, which are only in the infancy of the product. The severity of the Western climate, the absolute disaster to the farmer when a crop is lost, the cost of protecting stock and maintaining comfort in the long winters, and the great distance from the consuming centres of the country, all point to the productive lands, the genial climate, and the general prolific results of labor in the South as certain to make new highways for immigration and a new departure in the growth and development of the Southern States east of Kentucky and Mississippi. And of all these, Florida must certainly grow in favor as its climate and resources become better understood. The older portion of the State, embracing the highlands of which Tallahassee is the centre, is rich as any of the other cotton States, but is ragged and worn by the indolence and bad farming which belonged to slavery. Farming is so easy, and middling crops can be gathered with such a small amount of labor, that little is done in the way of improving the soil by diversity and succession of crops, and stock-growing is neglected because it would require one-fourth the labor and expenditure to make equal returns with stock-growing in the North and West. All the chief products of the Pennsylvania farm, with the exception of wheat, timothy, and clover, can be grown with about half the labor and with greater certainty in harvests, and to them can be added the long-fibred or sea-island cotton, tobacco, upland rice, with pears and peaches in perfection, and oranges with moderate results. But it is the new Florida that has been developed within the last few years that I regard as the most inviting part of the whole continent for the small farmer who can adapt himself to its climate and the simple but systematic method of culture that here produces the best results for labor to be found in any State of the Union. As yet its products are but imperfectly developed. While the orange alone is the most profitable of crops when wisely located and sensibly handled, there is no orange land that will not produce other semi-tropical fruits and vegetables in abundance, in from two to four crops each year, with corn and potatoes and the best grasses for the growth of stock, and it is admitted by the sugar-planters of Louisiana that the reclaimed lands of Florida will be the most productive and profitable sugar lands this side of Cuba. I have given this subject as careful personal observation and inquiry as was possible in a brief visit to the State ; and I feel fully warranted in the opinions I have expressed as to the climate, resources, products of labor, healthfulness, and rapid and permanent growth and prosperity of Florida.

FLORIDA'S RECLAIMED LANDS.

THE great impetus given to Florida within the last few years is chiefly due to the bold and practical business enterprise of Hamilton Disston, of Philadelphia. It has long been known that the most valuable lands of the State are flooded by a succession of lakes beginning with Lake Tohopekaliga at Kissimmee and the little lake of the same name a short distance to the northeast, and extending through Lakes Hatchenaha, Cypress, Kissimmee, thence by the Kissimmee River to· Lake Okeechobee, the largest body of water in any one State of the Union, and thence by canal to the point where the Caloosahatchee River has channel enough to carry these surplus waters to the Gulf of Mexico at Punta Rassa, or the mouth of the Caloosahatchee. This outlet is but little south of Charlotte Harbor, that is destined to be the leading coast-port for trade and travel to Cuba, as it is some five hours nearer Havana than Tampa, with better waters for commerce. The Peninsula Railroad, extending from Plant City, on the Tampa line, to Charlotte Harbor, has just been opened with imposing ceremonies, in which Governor Perry and other prominent men participated, and its completion opens the way for trade, travel, and settlers to one of the richest sections of the State, while the canals and straightened channels cut between the overflowing lakes by the Disston enterprise, open direct and easy water navigation from the Gulf at the mouth of the Caloosahatchee through the very heart of the extreme southern part of the State that is inhabited or inhabitable. South of Lake Okeechobee and the Caloosahatchee are the two counties of Monroe and Dade, containing the great Cypress Swamp and the Everglades, both of which extend to the end of the peninsula, and will probably never have anything more than irregular inhabitants at certain points on the coast.

It is no new idea that has been put into practical operation by the Disston company to reclaim the more than eight millions of acres which have long been known as the most productive and intrinsically valuable lands of the State. Public attention was attracted to the subject nearly forty years ago by General Jessup and other officers who had given long public service in Indian wars and as government engineers. General Jessup reported in 1848 that the drainage of these lands was entirely practicable, and that when drained they would become as valuable sugar plantations as any in the world. Government engineers subsequently proved what was then generally believed, that the glades are sufficiently elevated to be drained, and the careful and completed surveys of the Disston organization prove that there is a regular fall of nearly fifty feet from Kissimmee City, the head of the enterprise, to the Caloosahatchee, that is the outlet for the lakes when connected by canal between Lake Okeechobee and the river. The great lake had no visible outlet until opened by canal to carry its waters to the river, and to that canal will be added another on the east side, tapping the lake near its northeast corner and running eastward to the Atlantic coast at the confluence of the St. Lucie and the Halpotyokee Rivers. But while this body of land of almost incalculable value was well known to the South, and especially to its sugar-planters, its reclamation was never seriously thought of.

The planters of the South were too comfortable and contented in their condition, and too uncomfortable and discontented with the aggressive industry and enterprise of the North, to seek these lands before the war; and since the war the resources of the South, even with the freshly-infused energy among the people, have not been equal to the task of repairing the ravages of war, and, of course, could not consider an undertaking that required vast outlay of money and patient waiting for results. It was not until 1881 that the Atlantic and Gulf Coast Canal and Okeechobee Land Company was granted a special charter by the Florida Legislature, with an authorized capital of ten millions, and obtained a concession from the State, of undisputed lawful authority, for the reclamation of all lands lying south of Township Twenty-four and east of Peace Creek, embracing over eight millions of acres. By the concession made to the Disston corporation every alternate section reclaimed becomes the property of the company in fee simple without lien of any kind. The direction of the corporation is exclusively Philadelphian, with the exception of Samuel H. Gray, of Camden, and F. A. Hendry, of Florida.

The Philadelphians are Hamilton Disston, Charles H. Gross, William H. Wright, T. Henry Asbury, Lewis W. Klohr, John L. Hill, A. C. Haynes, James M. Kreamer, and Robert W. Gibson. They accepted a work of colossal proportions, but Mr. Disston, who is the chief capitalist and manager of the enterprise, wisely calculated the certain outcome, and he has already passed the point of doubt and can clearly see the rapidly-approaching consummation that must bring more than ample reward. When it is remembered that the work had to be begun in an unsettled portion of the State; that boats and machinery had to be constructed and operated for several years with no population but the operators of the company, and that various experiments had to be made under the severest trials before the proper methods could be mastered, the green verdure, fragrant blossoms, and bustling little city of Kissimmee, that has risen from the waters of the overflowing lake, must be a grateful spectacle to the men who made the gigantic venture; but there is more substantial satisfaction for them in the fact that they have been entirely successful in their theory and operations, and have already transferred to them in fee one million one hundred and fifty-five thousand four hundred and thirty-two acres of land, being one-half of the amount actually reclaimed thus far by their efforts.

After five years of often embarrassing operations by the Disston company, what was the generally accepted theory as to the intrinsic and early market value of the reclaimed lands has been conclusively demonstrated by the perfect reclamation and the luxuriant growth of valuable crops. These lake-border soils which are now, for the first time, accessible to cultivation, "are composed of humus, with a small percentage of sand and disintegrated marine deposits, underlaid by a stratum of shell marl,—the whole resting upon a coralline or limestone formation," as is stated in the description given of them in brief by Engineer Kreamer, and whether cultivated or not they employ their wealth of productive power in the most luxuriant growth. I spent a day on the head lake and the canal connecting it with its sister lake below, and inspecting the cultivated fields which two years ago were sporting-places for the magnificent fish which abound in these ever fresh waters. The tree that shades the farm-house on the inland side, at the

foot of the first lake, was until lately the object
to which the steamboat that bore me over the
broad lake was moored when carrying men and
materials to that point for the work; and the five-
hundred-acre farm of reclaimed land on which
Colonel Rose, assistant superintendent of the company, has his home, with its strawberries, which
I gathered in spite of the general destruction by
the severe winter, and its acres of blossoming vegetables and cabbages, soon to be marketed, attest
not only the complete success of the drainage enterprise, but also the exceptional value of the soil
rescued for the husbandman.   His farm, just wrested
from the bottom of the lake and with cultivation
and improvement only commenced, would sell for
more per acre to-day than half the best farms of
Chester County, for the simple reason that one
man and a mule can grow more from an acre
every four months than four men and as many
mules and acres could grow in Pennsylvania in a
year.   At the foot of the lake, where cultivation
has had only one full season to demonstrate the
fertility of the soil, I saw one cabbage-field, just
about ready to be cut, whose product will return
to the owner over twenty thousand dollars, and

then his land will be ready for another crop of whatever will pay best in season, without the possibility of needed fertilizers for many years. Besides it, where the steamboat sailed without obstruction only two years ago, I saw the product of the sugar-field from which was gathered the best cane exhibited at the New Orleans Exposition; and while the plant must be renewed every two years in the best lands of Louisiana, the near approach to the climate and soil of Cuba assures successive crops from year to year for probably a decade without replanting. I never appreciated until I saw this soil and its product, the truth and force of General Grant's letter on Florida, published in the *Public Ledger* several years ago, in which he said that the State "is capable of supplying all the oranges, lemons, pineapples, and other semi-tropical fruits used in the United States, and one hundred million dollars of sugar now imported." In the same letter he tersely and correctly summarized the resources of the State by saying that "it has an area greater than New York, Massachusetts, and Connecticut combined, with deposits of fertilizer under it and above it sufficient for many generations; it only wants people and enterprise,

16*

both of which it is rapidly obtaining, and it affords
the best opening in the world for young men of
small means and great industry." That this reclaimed section will become the great sugar centre
of the Union in a very few years is in no sense
doubtful; and when it is considered that much
less valuable sugar lands in Louisiana, because in
a much less friendly climate for the tender product, are worth from one to two hundred dollars
per acre, the prospective value of these Florida
lands may be measurably appreciated. They are
undoubtedly the best sugar lands of the world outside of Cuba, and the whole sugar belt of Florida
will have a great water highway to the Gulf as
a central artery of trade. By another year there
will be regular lines of boats from Kissimmee to
Charlotte Harbor, and thus this whole rich country
will offer every inducement of climate, soil, variety
of product, easy cultivation, and cheap transportation, through the only really tropical water channels
of the Union.

The reclaimed land of the Southern lake region
of Florida is not all sugar land. It presents every
variety of soil and growth common to the climate.
Back of the waters and rich bottom-lands what

are called the hammocks are abundant; the higher lands which are timbered with hard or soft woods according to the quality of soil. The live-oak, hickory, birch, sweet bay, palmetto, mangrove, and mastic are common; large bodies of cypress are within range of the new transportation just opened, and the pine lands are adapted to the orange grove. The chief advantage of this section of Florida is in the almost tropical climate, that exempts the fruit and vegetable crops from frosts when about Jacksonville and even farther south there is widespread destruction. From three to four crops can be grown each year, and there is no need of more than a single mule to plough to a proper depth, as there is no sod and no baking of the earth. Cotton, corn, sugar, tobacco, rice, potatoes, and very nutritious grasses for stock can be grown in the reclaimed lands, and the upland or hammock lands are the best of the continent for the orange grove excepting the Indian River country that is just east of the lake region on the Atlantic coast. The orange will bear several years earlier there than on the St. John's because of the more genial climate, and other crops are hastened in proportion. Strawberries can be gathered the same year they are planted; figs bear in two years from cuttings; grapes bear the second year, peaches the second or third year, and oranges in four years from the bud. In ten years from this time the reclaimed lake lands will present the richest and most productive and prosperous settlement of Florida unless all present experience and indications are at fault; and if its opportunities were properly understood by the large class of small farmers of the North who labor hard and unceasingly to gain only scant food and raiment with little enjoyment, there would be a sudden influx of new settlers. Why our young men who seek to gain farms in the West by patient industry and severe economy should risk the uncertainties of crops and be content with the slow advancement they can make there at best, when they can have cheaper lands, more easily cultivated lands, more accessible lands, greatly more productive lands, vastly more certainty in crops, with perpetual summer and less extreme of heat than there is in Iowa or Kansas, can be explained only by the want of general knowledge of the opportunities offered in Florida. I believe, as General Grant expressed it, that "Florida today affords the best opening in the world for young men of small means and great industry." Any intelligent man who comes and sees for himself will reach the same conclusion, and the most inviting part of Florida for men who come to make their homes here and get the best results of their own industry, is the large section now partially and soon to be completely reclaimed in the Southern lake region.

HINTS TO FLORIDA SETTLERS.

A SINGLE week is a short time in which to look over a State with as many imperfectly understood features as there are in Florida. I don't pretend to have done anything approaching justice to the subject; but I have traversed the St. John's from Jacksonville to Sanford, a distance of nearly two hundred miles; have travelled between the same points by rail; have journeyed southward by rail from Sanford fifty miles to Kissimmee, and spent a day on the lakes and reclaimed lands which skirt them; have seen the Atlantic coast at venerable St. Augustine and the northern part of the State from Jacksonville through Tallahassee to Pensacola, and have noted and studied with care the features of climate and product which chiefly interest the surplus capital and industry of the North. With the exception of one day given to a journey in the northern part of the State from the eastern sea to the western gulf, that is simply the

southern fringe of Georgia, I have devoted my time
to observation and inquiry in regard to the newer
and more southern region that is now, and must
long continue to be, the central attraction for
Northern investors and settlers. The early settlers
from the North naturally located on the romantic
banks of the St. John's, as there was no transportation southward except that furnished by the great
river that is a law unto itself in flowing its waters
toward the North Star. On its green shores are
beautiful winter homes, with orange groves, early
vegetation, a profusion of heartsome shrubbery and
fragrant flowers; but the winter frosts are expected
annually with more or less severity, and the growth
of oranges and early vegetables is an incident rather
than a purpose. The banks of the great river and
its succession of fresh lakes are spangled with towns
which are supported mainly by winter sojourners,
and settlers have logically followed the embryo cities.
The largest and best cultivated orange groves of the
State are close to the St. John's,—one hundred miles
or more south of Jacksonville, and they are sources
of immense profit even with the peril of frequent
frosts. Had the country for nearly two hundred
miles farther south, from Sanford, the chief southern

point of business on the river, to Lake Okeechobee, been opened by rail and boat ten years ago as it is now, the great orange groves would be there and practically safe from the ravages of winter, as they are on the Indian River. It is to this new part of Florida just opened to settlement by the railroad from Sanford, southwest to the Gulf at Tampa and also to Charlotte Harbor, and by water through the Disston drainage system, traversing the interior lands to the mouth of the Caloosahatchee, that the attention of investors and settlers must now be directed. By these improvements millions of acres of the best lands in the best climate of the State have been made inviting to settlers, as they present all the advantages of the earlier settled northern section, with more productive soil and as nearly a tropical climate as can be found in any part of the continent that is inhabitable. I have observed this section hastily and studied it imperfectly of course, but sufficiently to reach correct general conclusions, and I will close my observations and suggestions by a few practical hints to those who contemplate investing or settling in Florida.

While there are other portions of the State which offer great inducements to both capital and labor, the tide of both money and population will certainly go south of Sanford for years to come, and I believe that the more fortunate will be fifty miles or more south of Kissimmee. The rapid growth of thriving towns and beautiful farms along the line of the railway from Sanford to Kissimmee, and the rapid increase of the value of lands, prove not only how Northern settlers get as far south as possible within range of transportation, but how rapidly and substantially population and wealth multiply. Now the railway is open for the first time from Sanford clear through to Tampa, striking the Gulf south of the 28th degree, and only opened in March to Charlotte Harbor south of the 27th degree. These railways drain the products of the Gulf side of Southern Florida, and the water highway just about to be opened through the Disston system of connecting canals and lakes will drain the products of the Ocean side, and both traverse the centre of their respective sections. This region would have been preferred by early settlers even if the present severest winter for half a century had not given an admonition on the subject that none can fail to heed; but with the whole orange crop remaining on the trees and the entire crop of early vegetables destroyed by the freeze of last January, all doubts will be resolved in favor of the lands farthest south which are productive and accessible to rail or water highways. This region has been so lately open to investment and settlement that it is virgin soil for both, and is much cheaper than any other lands of equal fertility and advantages to be found in the State. I don't hesitate to advise, therefore, that present investments in Florida for either actual settlers or for speculative profit, as a rule, should be made in the newly-opened southern section of the State. Both settlers and speculators can easily make mistakes there as elsewhere in a new country, but I believe that there is the very minimum of risk in the belt of the peninsula extending from midway between the 29th and 28th degrees to the 27th. This takes in the Indian River and the reclaimed lands of the interior lakes, and there will be the centre of productive wealth in the Land of Flowers.

Speculators need no advice about the purchase of lands, nor is it a matter of special public interest whether they are successful or unsuccessful in their ventures; but actual settlers need to be well and practically advised, and their success or failure is a matter of vital interest to both the community and the State. There may be many speculative operations in Florida which will be fruitful mainly in disappointment, and there will be many actual settlers who, from some of the many obstacles which ever confront immigrants in new homes, will fail in Florida; but, as a rule, it will be the fault of the settler, and not the fault of the climate, soil, or possibilities of the country. One of the common mistakes of agricultural immigrants is the belief that they must have as large a farm here as they would need in Pennsylvania, where they must devote half of their land and labor to keeping themselves and their stock during the unproductive more than half the year. A farm of twenty acres properly located in Florida is equal to a farm of sixty acres in the North in producing capacity, and no part of the farm or labor is necessary to sustain either family or stock in unproductive seasons, as there are no non-producing periods from January until January. The settler who is to depend upon his own industry and economy to acquire a home must have eighty or more acres anywhere in the West, but twenty acres of fertile soil in the newly-opened Florida region can be bought for less money per acre than any land of equal fertility, transportation, and cheapness of improvement west of the Father of Waters, and in three or four months' time, and steadily thereafter, he can feed himself and all he possesses from his own soil with comparatively little labor, excepting only his wheat bread and groceries. Forty acres are more than any farmer who expects to do the chief part of his own work can farm with profit in Florida, and the man who farms half the amount well will do better than his neighbor who attempts to farm more. When it is considered that one acre of first-class vegetable soil in a nearly tropical climate will generally produce more than the best twenty-acre field of wheat in Pennsylvania, and that some profitable crop can be repeated in the ground at least three times a year, the importance of small farms and good farming may be appreciated. Even the grasses on which stock can be as well fed as on our clover- and timothy-fields of Pennsylvania, need only a few weeks to make sweet and nutritious pastures, and the little hay required to keep stock in the best condition is hardly to be taken into the account of the general labor of the farm. Stock is badly cared for in most parts of the State only because it can come so nearly maintaining itself that the regulation Southern farmer allows it to take its chances for the whole season, much to his own loss. What I wish to impress upon young men who want to work themselves into the ownership of a home and a farm that will afford them a good living with reasonably-assured profits is, that while they must have sixty or eighty acres in the West to do so, they will be as well provided with land, for practical results, with twenty acres in the southern portion of Florida; and land of the best producing qualities is now cheaper per acre in that region than is land of like qualities and advantages of market in any desirable portion of the West. A small farmer would do well to buy forty acres in Florida to multiply the future profits of his labors, but if he farms ten of it well the first year and twenty of it in five years, he will accomplish a great work and have a small fortune in his untouched lands.

Many Northern settlers will be slow to learn that it is a great transformation from the rigorous climate of the North to the almost tropical climate of Southern Florida, and those who refuse to understand the common-sense laws which require reasonable adaptation of habit and diet to climate will suffer thereby.

There is nothing to apprehend from the popular bugbear of malaria in Florida, if any measure of care is exercised in selecting a location. It will be more difficult to make such a mistake in Florida than it would be in Pennsylvania or Kansas, but it can be made. The chief peril to the health of Northern settlers in Florida is in their own neglect of the plain laws of nature which the commonest comprehension should understand and obey. The savage of the Arctic region lives and thrives on blubber, and even the Arctic navigator can relish a dish of oil that would be applied only to his coarse boots or harness at home; but neither savage nor navigator would live a month in Florida on such diet, any more than they would live if clad for an Arctic winter in a semi-tropical climate. The Northern settler transferred into a Florida climate must accept the lighter, cheaper, and in every way better diet that nature offers him. Fruits and vegetables, so abundant around him, must largely take the place of his strong meats, greasy cakes, and generally heavy dishes which make the system feverish with needless heat even in the North, or his liver will become sluggish, bilious disorders will be bred, and general ill health imputed to the climate, when it is solely the fault of the sufferer himself. While the extreme of heat in Florida, even in what is the nearest approach to a tropical climate that can be settled, is not as great as that of Philadelphia, the almost perpetual summer requires for both immigrants and natives lighter food and more care to avoid exhaustive exertion; but there is no reason why residents should become enervated. There is vastly more suffering from Northern diet in Florida than from malaria; and when it is considered that Florida only imperiously exacts the diet that common sense suggests in the North, there should be willing obedience to the laws of health in this region.

The cost of purchasing and outfitting a farm in the section of Florida to which the bulk of immigration will turn its steps is much less than in any part of the West that is at all inviting to settlers. While lands in the thickly-populated and well-improved parts of the State along the lines of transportation are as dear as they are in Chester County, the more fertile and more certainly productive lands now just opened farther south can be purchased in good locations for ten dollars per acre, and they are about as cheaply prepared for cultivation as the heavy-sodded prairie-lands of the West, which require a year of taming before they produce at all. When once brought under cultivation one mule is abundant for the best of ploughing, and no heavy teams are necessary for hauling. Buildings are erected much cheaper than in Pennsylvania, as lumber is abundant, being one of the chief products of the State. An outlay of twenty-five hundred dollars would buy a forty-acre farm, build a comfortable house, procure stock and implements, and put one-fourth the farm in first-class cultivation, with an orange grove in the ground. No barns are needed, as hay is stacked and stock require little protection at any season of the year. Half that amount can be had on credit on the land and improvements, but at double the rate of interest that like good security would command in the North. This estimate is for what would be a large farm for one who expects to cultivate it himself, and for what would be regarded as good improvements; but those whose necessities will accept the pinching self-denial of a majority of Western immigrants can start small farms on little capital except industry and economy, and they can live comfortably all the year on their own products after the first four months. In short, the small farmer, or the young man who seeks to earn a home and farm for himself, has every advantage of climate, cheapness and fertility of soil, early and bountiful product, and easy market facilities in Southern Florida, and it is undoubtedly the most inviting part of the Union now open to young men whose fortune is in their stout hearts and willing hands.

THE SUGAR INDUSTRY.

THE sugar-planting interest is limited to four States, of which Louisiana is the chief, with Mississippi and Texas furnishing small belts now devoted to that industry, and the new and most promising Florida sugar belt just about to be opened to cultivation. In Louisiana it is the main product, and has more capital invested in it, outside of the sugar lands, than is invested in all the cotton States for the cultivation and marketing of cotton, exclusive of the soil. The cotton plantation can be stocked at a comparatively small outlay, including the cotton-gin, but to stock a good sugar plantation requires an investment of not less than one hundred and fifty thousand dollars in machinery and appliances for the growth and marketing of the crop. With an outlay on each first-class sugar plantation equal to a first-class anthracite furnace in Pennsylvania, a failure of the crop or

a severe depression in the market must greatly
paralyze the business of Louisiana. With the
sugar-planters prosperous, Louisiana is prosperous; with the sugar-planters unfortunate from any
cause, there is general stagnation and embarrass-
ment throughout the State. The commerce of New
Orleans does not depend upon the single product
of sugar, as the commerce of Mobile, Savannah,
and Charleston depends upon cotton; but while
the Crescent City draws largely upon the cotton
of the Southern States, reached by the Mississippi,
and upon the products of Northern and Western
States, drained by the Father of Waters and its
tributaries, sugar is the chief source of productive
wealth in Louisiana, and the mere commerce of
a port cannot revive the general depression caused
by unsuccessful sugar-planting. No centre of commerce or trade can prosper in a State when there
is a general absence of prosperity among the great
producing interests. This is very clearly illustrated
in Louisiana at this time. The sugar-planting interests are prostrated to a degree not experienced
at any time since the war, and there is little prospect of an immediate revival of the industry that
is so important to this State. Few sugar-planters

have paid actual expenses, even with severely economical management, for the last year; a large
majority have lost money, and I hear of none
who have profit after expenses and taxes, not
counting interest on the heavy capital required.

The problem of continuing or annihilating the
sugar industry of the South, is one that presents
peculiarly embarrassing features for our statesmanship. We are now paying some fifty millions annually in tariff duties to protect little more than
one-tenth that amount of product; and as sugar
enters into the daily consumption of all classes,
rich and poor, the continuance of a protective policy
is naturally antagonized, even outside of free-trade
theorists, by considerations of interest. After all
our theories about protection and free-trade, we all
want to get the most we can for our own products, and want to buy the products of others as
cheaply as possible. The question of interest is,
therefore, the underlying principle that impels different sections with different industries to help or hinder
conflicting theories of statesmanship. The Pennsyl-
vanian wants protection for iron and for coal and
for the products of factories; the cotton-planter
of the South, who buys everything he consumes

and sells his whole harvest without importing competition, wants free-trade; and the sugar- and rice-
planters who skirt the cotton-fields toward the
coast want protection, and they must have it or
abandon the utterly unequal contest with foreign
producers. Large as the protection now is for sugar,
it is inadequate to the maintenance of the sugar
industry. Under the special fostering care of their
governments, the sugar-producers of Germany,
France, and Spain can now undersell our domestic
sugar, with nearly two cents a pound of duty in
our favor; and with the perfection of science applied
to the product in foreign governments, and the
largest percentage of sugar obtained from the raw
material because of government guarantee, there is
little prospect of anything like equality of advantages between the domestic and foreign sugar-producers. - Like the advancement in the production
of steel, by which the product has been cheapened
more than fifty per cent. within a few years,
the advancement in the production of sugar, by
the refinement of mechanism, has cheapened the
product nearly fifty per cent. abroad. Germany
has advanced from the production of three per
cent. of sugar from the beet to thirteen per cent.;

France has advanced in almost equal proportion, and Cuba has kept pace with her competing sugar-fields to multiply and cheapen the product. This has been done in Germany and France by lavish subsidies to sugar-producers, in shape of drawbacks on importations. Sugar is more costly to the consumers of Germany and France than it is to the consumers of the United States, as the home consumption is heavily taxed; but liberal drawbacks of taxes on all importations of sugar, and the fixed and permanent guarantee of the government to the sugar-producer, warrants the employment of the most improved machinery to reach the largest percentage of product. The Louisiana sugar-planters have increased the product by recent improvements in machinery from five to seven and eight per cent., but they could increase it to ten or twelve per cent. by improvements already tested, and they must do it or give up the battle. To compete with the protected sugar-growers of foreign countries our home sugar-planters must practically throw out their present machinery as old iron, although costing from one hundred thousand to one hundred and fifty thousand dollars on each large plantation, and supplant it with the equally costly but perfected machinery lately applied to the sugar industry. They would do so if they had the guarantee of permanent protection from the government that is given abroad,—that is, the protection that would enable them to meet the foreign producers on equal terms as to profit. They have not that protection now; they have no assurance that the present protection will be continued, and they can venture on no new experiments as costly as all improvements in sugar production are with an uncertain Tariff policy. These facts explain why the sugar-planters of the South are suffering the severest paralysis in their industry, and why they cannot make new outlay to improve their product.

The country must now look the fact squarely in the face, that we must largely and permanently protect the sugar industry or let it be entirely effaced from the list of American products. If the industry is to be fostered, it must have either increased protection by Tariff duties, or it must have a certain subsidy for a definite period long enough to develop it in the appliances necessary to the largest percentage of product. To remove the Tariff on sugar would at once blot out our surplus revenue, and to offer a subsidy sufficient to develop the

industry to a self-sustaining point would require a
present annual draft upon the revenue of ten millions, to be increased each year for the period of
ten years,—the shortest period named as sufficient
to enable our sugar-producers to compete with the
world. The theory of the most intelligent sugar-
planters I have met is that the guarantee of four
cents a pound upon sugar for ten years, either by
Tariff duty or by government subsidy, would enable
them thereafter to undersell the world, and establish
one of the most important and prosperous and self-
supporting industries of the continent. I doubt not
that less protection than they name would as fully
accomplish the purpose; but I give the theory of
those best informed and most interested, and I
look upon it with interest and favor because any
industry that can be made self-sustaining and seek
the markets of the world, by a season of protection, cheapens products for future consumers and
adds to the common wealth of the whole country.
I do not assume to decide how the problem of
saving the sugar industry of the South is to be
solved; but I am clear that it should be saved;
and if it is to be saved from utter annihilation, it
is cheapest and best for all, for producer and con-

sumer alike, that it be so saved as to quicken it to the earliest and highest perfection in cheapness and percentage of product. It is an industry that cannot long languish, for in languishing it must die, because of the exceptional cost of the plant; and the country must decide at an early day whether we shall pay for a season to assure the cheap production of our own sugar, for which we have ample fields, or pay from one hundred and fifty million to two hundred million dollars annually to the sugar-growers of foreign lands. If a subsidy of five hundred millions would give England an abundant and cheaper supply of cotton, India would command it without a voice of protest. While ostensibly a free-trade government because of interest, no nation of the world more lavishly protects the industries essential to her internal revenue and general prosperity than does England.

THE NEGRO AS A RULER.

THE problem of negro self-rule has not been solved, as the true solution must be the work of years of opportunity for growth in fitness for it, but it has been fairly tried in two portions of the Union since the war, and in both instances it has resulted in debauched leaders and demoralized followers, leaving the general condition of the race worse because of the experiment. To assume that the black man, who has been a slave in the South and a menial in the North, and whose education was either positively interdicted or neglected, should prove himself proficient in self-rule, without aid or even sympathy from the mass of the whites, is to judge him by a standard that would overthrow every principle of popular government; but a country that is struggling to solve the problem of universal suffrage, with great States subject to the numerical majority of ignorant and thriftless masses, must carefully study every recurring phase of the effort. In Washington City, where the negro was first enfranchised, the nation exhibited to the world the most corrupt, profligate, and demoralized government to be found in the Union, and the same political power that gave the ballot to the black men of the capital, was compelled to revoke the elective franchise and save the credit and good name of Washington by making the negro voiceless in his own government. It was a sad necessity,—and a sad confession of the failure of suffrage when exercised by race prejudice without intelligence; but the same Republican statesmen who gave the right of self-rule to the black man in the capital of the nation, had to rescue the capital from destruction and shame by sweeping disfranchisement.

In no section of the Union did the colored race have such an opportunity to succeed in creditable self-rule as in South Carolina, and the failure has simply made it impossible for them to regain power in that State for many years to come. That the illiterate bondman of yesterday should rule a great State wisely to-day could not be expected; but the masses have failed to be just to themselves and to the power they were suddenly called upon to exercise, mainly because of the corruption and faithless-

ness of the leaders of the race. South Carolina had
a galaxy of colored leaders when reconstruction
committed the control of the State to the preponder-
ating race, that has not been equalled in ability and
culture in the race in any other portion of the
country; and if they had been honest with their
race and with power, the negro masses would have
been elevated, instead of demoralizing them, and they
would have been taught industry, self-reliance, and
thrift instead of appealing to the passions, prejudices,
and low cupidity of ignorance. When I recall the
long list of able negroes who were prominent in the
early Republican rule of South Carolina and follow
them through their gradual descent into dependence
or shame, it presents a pointed commentary upon
the problem of self-rule by the negro. There are
negro names connected with the control of South
Carolina which should have made the State and the
race illustrious in the elevation of the freedmen and
in the just government of the Commonwealth. And
many of them were natives of the State. Cardoza,
Rainey, Smalls, and Nash were all born in slavery.
Cardoza was made free by his father-master; Rainey
purchased his own freedom before the war, and
Smalls and Nash were made free by emancipation.

These men, endowed with uncommon intelligence and knowing the bondman's cruel life, should have been each a Moses to lead his people into the promised land of self-rule; but Cardoza and Smalls are convicts, and Nash escaped the criminal dock by confession and resignation of his seat in the Senate. Rainey alone escaped a career of crime, and he ceased to be potential with his race. Of the other distinguished negro leaders I recall the untutored but eloquent Whipper, who came from Michigan; the shrewd and unscrupulous Purvis, who bore an honored Philadelphia name; the brilliant Elliott, who fitted himself in the free schools of Massachusetts to answer the Confederate Ex-Vice President Stephens in triumph on the floor of Congress; the lawyer, Wright, who was the first negro admitted to the bar in Pennsylvania, and who rose to the Supreme Bench of South Carolina; the cultured Delany, who won college honors in Ohio, and once made a bold stand for negro reform by running as the reform candidate for Lieutenant-Governor, and the sagacious Boseman, who served his race by nestling down as the Charleston postmaster. There were others of more or less ability, but the half-score I have named should have made South Carolina a most prosperous Commonwealth and her numerical majority of freedmen a happy and wisely self-ruled people.

The man who should have been the foremost of his race in honor and usefulness is Cardoza. He had everything to make him faithful and eminent. He possesses superior natural abilities, was thoroughly educated in Scotland when nominally a slave, entered the ministry and was the respected pastor of a New England congregation when emancipation and reconstruction brought him back to aid his people in the escape from darkness. He came with the purest and loftiest aims, and was the first Secretary of State under the carpet-bag reign. He was purposely assigned to that position by the ruling white and black adventurers because he was honest, as his official duties gave him no power of restraint upon his thieving associates; but the luxury of crime was around him on every side; he learned to tolerate it, and soon his good purposes were lost in the flood-tide of corruption that surged against him. He was deemed sufficiently demoralized to be made State Treasurer under the later and more violent reign of debauchery, and he ended a convict. He was saved from sentence by the general treaty of peace between the contending forces of the State that saved Patterson, Smalls, and Nash, with Cardoza, from the penitentiary; gave Butler his seat in the United States Senate, and ended various Federal prosecutions for violation of the national election laws. Cardoza became a clerk under the Hayes administration. Whipper was one of the earliest of the legislative jobbers, and succeeded in foisting himself into a judicial election, but both sides revolted against such a mockery of justice, and he was compelled to surrender his claim to the office. He is now a local leader and pettifogger among the semi-barbarous negro hordes of Beaufort. Purvis was a prominent leader in the House as chairman of a most important committee, and he did as much as any one to hasten the overthrow of negro rule. He resides in Charleston, and became a beneficiary of the national government. Elliott is one of the ablest and boldest of the race I have known. He gathered a fair education in the Massachusetts free schools, and developed into one of the most brilliant and sagacious leaders of the State. He was Adjutant-General, Speaker of the House and Member of Congress, and his famous debate with Alexander H. Stephens in the national House of Representatives stamped

him as capable of high leadership among men. But
he devoted his great abilities to the work of plunder
instead of elevating and benefiting his race, and
when the State was robbed until both whites and
blacks were impoverished, the deluded negroes deserted him, and he then basked in the sunshine of
a department position in Washington. Wright had
a rare opportunity to make a creditable record for
himself, his race, and his adopted State. He had
opened the way for the elevation of his colored
brethren by gaining the first admission to the bar
in Pennsylvania, and he was chosen one of the three
Supreme Judges of South Carolina. He was not
eminently fitted for the position, although he could
have filled it creditably by the exercise of judicial
integrity, but his decisions soon became a matter of
open barter, and dissipation followed his disgrace,
until he finally resigned to escape unanimous im-
peachment. Smalls is of the heroic mould. He
is remembered as the slave who ran his vessel into
the Union blockade to cast his fortunes with the
defenders of the government. He is illiterate, of
course, but a man of rare natural abilities. He should
have been a beacon-light for his race to guide them
to advancement, industry, and honest thrift, but he

ended his career in State politics as a convict and carried his dishonor into Congress. Nash was an illiterate hotel servant in Columbia before the war, but he had much of the ability and more of the selfish cunning of Smalls, and he was an omnipotent local leader for a time, making himself Senator and Presidential elector in 1876. He held the fate of Hayes in his hands when the result in the State was questioned, and he made the most of it. He publicly professed to have received a large offer from the Democrats to vote for Tilden, but whites and blacks understood that it was simply notice that the Republicans must pay his price, and it had to be done. He confessed his guilt as a Senator and resigned to save prosecution, and he is now in obscure retirement with none so poor as to do him reverence. Boseman made a battle for himself and became comfortably fixed as postmaster in Charleston, and Delany was a trial justice by the favor of the Democratic Governor. Rainey purchased his own freedom, and has been active in the Republican control of the State without becoming noted as a jobber. He was assailed as corrupt, but it was because he tolerated rather than participated in corruption, and the searching investigation that fol-

lowed the overthrow of the carpet-baggers failed
to stamp him with guilt, but he has lost his power
with his race because he is regarded as a place-
man, and he gravitated to a Washington clerkship.
Such is the sad story of the decline or fall of the
ablest body of negro leaders ever felt in any of
the States.

None know better than the masses of the colored
voters of South Carolina that their attempt at self-
rule has been a terrible failure, and they are now
distrustful of all colored leaders, while they have
nothing but curses for the desperate white adventurers who impoverished both races while assuming
to elevate and benefit the negro. It was this feeling
that made the election of Hampton possible in 1876,
and the sceptre once wrested from such a race will
not soon be regained. They feel little hope of aiding
themselves by a negro restoration. They saw the
State robbed of lands for negro homes, and the
property stolen by those who claimed to be the friend
of the negro. They saw taxes wrung from property
to educate the negro, and a large portion stolen out-
right, and the schools made merely a mockery of
education. Now they see seventy-five thousand
colored children in free-schools, and nearly twelve

hundred colored teachers instructing them under the
beneficence of the State. They see, also, an amendment of the Constitution adopted making fixed and
irrevocable appropriations for free and equal education, and the Governor of the State declaring for still
greater increase in the facilities for instructing both
whites and blacks. They see business and confidence revive; they have more labor and better pay;
they are steadily increasing their friendly relations
with the whites by leases of lands, and many of them
are becoming small proprietors since they have
ceased to neglect industry to follow the commands of
selfish leaders, and a large proportion of the more
thrifty class have openly taken their political stand
with the whites, while thousands of others, especially in minority counties, refuse to take any part in
politics. They have a majority of from twenty to
thirty thousand in the State on a strict color-line
division, but there will never be another solid negro
vote cast in this State. Superior intelligence and
will must rule here as in all other places in the
world, and both whites and blacks understand it.
There will be unjustifiable methods to repress such
negro counties as Beaufort and Charleston, and they
will need the correcting hand of justice; but until all

the laws of human nature and of interest shall be reversed, the white man will rule the inferior race, and he will do it better in the South at this time than the negro can rule himself. This is not the sentimental view of the race issue in the South, but it is the truth.

THE RACE PROBLEM.

THE first serious phase of the race problem in the South has been solved; but its solution is likely to present another and a graver problem, involving the two races of the South. After years of fretful strife, made mainly by adventurers who appealed to the ignorance, prejudice, and cupidity of the blacks, the whites rule the entire South, with the active co-operation of a considerable number of the more intelligent and thrifty blacks, and with the entirely passive assent of the others. Here, as elsewhere in the Union, and as elsewhere in every civilization of the world, intelligence, integrity, and property, when combined, will inevitably rule in the end; and the battle of the blacks for political mastery, even if honestly and wisely led, could have attained only fitful triumphs. As it was most corruptly and unscrupulously led, without fidelity to either whites or blacks, and without respect for the interests of party

or race, defeat came speedily in disregard of all the
power and appliances of the national government,
and when it came it left only monuments of shame
for friend and foe. The profligacy and theft of negro
rule in the South alienated the few of the race who
saw that freedom did not furnish corn and bacon,
and that blacks, like whites, must earn their own
bread by the sweat of the brow; and others soon
learned that the bewildering promises of adventurers
who organized and voted the blacks were made to
the ear only to be broken to the hope. The result
has logically been that as negroes became indus-
trious and thrifty and the owners of property, they
have either voted with the whites to assure the safety
of both person and property, or they have retired
from all participation in politics. There is nothing
novel in this feature of the race question in the
South. The blacks of the South are employed and
fed almost wholly by the property-owners, and they
have everything to lose by political antagonism. In
the North, and in no Northern State more than in
Pennsylvania, tens of thousands of intelligent whites
vote with their employers for the same reasons, and
many of them would suffer the same fate as the
blacks of the South if they voted against the capital

that gives them labor. The same immutable law that governs the political relations between employers and employed in the North governs in the South, only it governs a much larger measure of intelligence and pride of manhood in Pennsylvania than in Alabama. If intelligent citizens of any Northern State will look about them among their own people in a political campaign, they will see the clear explanation of what is called the failure of the black vote of the South. It is the question of corn and bacon in the South; it is the question of bread and raiment in the North, and that tells the whole story.

The political revolution that retired the Republican party from power, after a reign of nearly a quarter of a century, will end all effort at political organization on the race line. It has been practically a failure for years past, when there were many circumstances to inspire the hope of partial success; and now the whole race issue perishes by the change of national authority. To-day there is nothing left of the race organization in politics. There was a shudder among the blacks immediately after the election of Cleveland, because they feared the fulfilment of the predictions of their leaders that they would be remanded back to slavery; but they already see that their leaders were deliberately untruthful, and all apprehensions of harshness to their race because of a change of political power have perished. Every possible appeal was made to their ignorance and prejudice before the late election, as has been usual in all election campaigns of the last fifteen years, to consolidate the colored vote as the only way to defeat a return to bondage; but now Democratic success has come; the whites have in no degree changed their friendly relations toward the blacks, and there are few of the colored race so ignorant as not to understand that no change in political authority can limit their civil rights. The blacks are, therefore, satisfactorily assured on the one question that disturbed them, and that assurance has taught them more pointedly than ever before that their leaders are characterless, untruthful, and dangerous to the peace and prosperity of the colored race. And when it is considered that the active leaders of the colored voters in maintaining the race issue in politics have been the Federal officials in the South, the end of race organization must be clearly apparent to all.

I have not seen an intelligent politician or business man in the South who does not look upon the

now assured general division of the colored voters
with grave apprehension. The race issue in politics,
although largely broken in recent elections, coerced
the practical unity of the whites. The conflicts of
ambition were subordinated to the common peril of
negro supremacy, and the whites were compelled
to stand together to avert it. There was no field
for free lancers in politics among the whites, and
their jealousies and conflicting aims were suppressed
by a supreme necessity to which all bowed without
question. Now the issue of black unity and of
black supremacy is an issue of the past. The colored voters will be indifferent to politics, as a rule,
except when appeals to their ambition and cupidity recall them to active efforts. The field is thus
opened to the long - smothered ambition of the
whites who would gladly have rudely jostled each
other in the race for promotion, and the blacks will
be appealed to by disputing aspirants. These appeals will not be made to the intelligence or to the
integrity of the blacks, as such appeals would be
profitless. They will be made to their ignorance,
to their prejudices, to their cupidity, to all their
baser qualities, just as ambitious politicians do in
the North, and there is grave danger of thus in-

augurating a general sweep of political demoralization in both races. The Southern people possess
just the same human nature that other people possess. They are likely to be just as ambitious and
as mean in promoting mean ambition as the average
American politician in every section of the country;
and with an immense colored vote, nearly equalling
the whites in many Southern States and superior
in numbers in South Carolina and Mississippi, and
in the lowest strata of ignorance, idleness, and su-
perstition, what must be the harvest of the obliter-
ation of the race line in Southern politics? This is
the most serious race problem the South has ever
attempted to solve, and I share the apprehensions
of the more intelligent Southern people that the
last stage of the race issue will be vastly worse
than any of the past.

There is much unreasonable misconception in the
North of the relative condition of the blacks in the
North and in the South. The prejudice of caste is
just equally strong in both sections of the country.
The black man can no more sit at the table of the
most blatant Republican in the North than he can
sit at the table of his old master in the South.
The same social laws govern all peoples, and they

are immutable. Politicians theorize differently in
election campaigns, but there the theory ends. The
prejudice of race is fivefold stronger in the North than
in the South. The Northern people have no love
for the black man, and even those who battled for
his freedom and enfranchisement, as a rule, cherish
vastly more profound prejudice of race than do the
Southern people. While the North maintains its
deep prejudice of race, the people of the South
have a general and strong sympathy for the negro.
Nearly all of them have played with the negro in
childhood, have been nursed by the black " mamma,"
and have grown up with more or less affection for
them. Classify it in what type of affection you
may, it is none the less an affection that tempers
the hard, unyielding prejudice of race that prevails
in the North. This distinction between the Northern and Southern people on the race question will
prepare the public mind in the North for the dissipation of another unfounded sectional prejudice that
is deeply rooted there. The educational facilities for
the blacks are better in the South to-day than they
are in the North, in proportion to the facilities proffered to all. South Carolina employs and pays out
of the State Treasury more black teachers than

are employed in all the States of the North, and
Alabama employs eleven hundred colored male
teachers and five hundred colored female teachers.
And they provide the best means for fitting the
colored people for teaching. The normal schools
for whites and blacks in both Alabama and South
Carolina are exactly equal, and the treasury of the
State is largely drawn upon to qualify the colored
race for teaching itself. North Carolina, Georgia,
Mississippi, and indeed most of the old slave States,
each sustain more colleges for the blacks than do
Pennsylvania or Massachusetts; and just as educational facilities have increased for the whites, whether
in common or normal schools or in colleges, they
have been equally increased for the blacks so far as
State appropriations have aided them. In Georgia
the colored University ranks with the white University, and even in Mississippi, presumably the
most Bourbon of Southern States, the State does
much more for the collegiate education of the black
race than does Pennsylvania. I have heard Southern men complain of many features of their local
governments, but I have yet to hear the first one to
complain of the equal education of the two races.
And what is true in the matter of education is

equally true of the recognition of the black race in Southern politics. I have seen colored Democratic members in the South Carolina Legislature, nominated and elected mainly by white votes, and in New Orleans the black policeman, appointed by Democratic authority, is met on every street and has worn the insignia of police power for years before a Democratic Mayor in Philadelphia first recognized the colored voter as entitled to wear the star and blue. In South Carolina alone there are more black Democrats in representative office than there are blacks of all parties in all the States of the North. Pennsylvania and Philadelphia, where the black voters hold the balance of power in both city and State, could not elect a colored man to the Legislature or to any other honorable or lucrative office in the strongest Republican district; but South Carolina Democrats elect him to office, with all the lingering prejudices of the relation of master and slave. The intelligent and dispassionate Northerner who closely observes the relations of the two races North and South, is forced to confess that with all our boasted superior devotion to the black race, and with all our assaults upon the South for the oppression of the blacks, the negro is better treated

by the South than by the North. I regret to make
such a confession; but it is the plain truth that we
theorize about the elevation of the black race with
little practice in accord with our teaching, while the
South theorizes little on the subject and practises
more than it teaches in the considerate care of the
emancipated slaves.

This is the plain truth in regard to race domination in the South, as it is the plain truth of the race
in the North. In the South every channel of industry is open to him. The white and the black
mechanic are on equal footing; the prejudices of race
have no existence, save when there is a struggle for
the domination of the spoiler over property, and he
legislates and fills positions for which he is fitted,
not only with the sympathy but often by the votes
of the whites. I saw black men sitting on the Democratic side of Southern Legislatures, but no Republican district in Philadelphia or Pennsylvania
has ventured to nominate one of the seventy-five
hundred colored voters of the city, or one of the
thrice that number in the State, for any legislative
position, either State or National. I saw the colored
man mingle with Democratic organizations in the
South, but not one could sit in the councils of the

League or the Union Club, or march in mixed ranks
with the Invincibles or Young Republicans in Philadelphia. I saw him have free access to every channel of mechanical industry in the South, but he is
relentlessly excluded from the organized mechanical
pursuits of Republican Philadelphia. His admission
into the printing-office of the *Times* or the *Press* or
the *North American* would vacate every white man's
case, where most of them vote the Republican ticket
to help the black man; and the colored labor of the
South, as a class, is to-day better paid, more steadily
employed, and more uniformly free from want than
the farm labor of the North or of any country of the
world. Indeed, so great is the demand for labor in
the now rapidly progressing South, that colored
laborers are employed from January to January as
a rule; their wives and children double or quadruple
their income in the cotton-picking season, that lasts
three months in the year, and there is now a yearly
winter influx of white labor from the North to aid in
the sugar and rice harvests. This is the peace to the
black and the white man that has followed the now
accepted domination of the whites in the South, and
the black man does not wish it changed for a renewal of a struggle to which he is utterly unequal.

If the North must assume the task of elevating the
black man to equal power regardless of fitness, let it
begin by giving him in Philadelphia, Pennsylvania,
New York, and other States the same industrial
equality and political promotion that the less educated blacks of the South now enjoy with the cordial
sympathy of the Southern whites. I saw the same
colored leader (ex-Senator Revels), who was excluded from the forum of the Academy of Music
when a Republican United States Senator, solely because of his race, now at the head of a colored college that is sustained entirely by the Democratic
State government of Mississippi, and he holds his
high commission from the same authority, while Republican Pennsylvania has no such temple of learning
for the black man. Although forbidden to speak in
the Philadelphia Academy, he can speak to intelligent and appreciative white audiences in the State
that is blotted by the Kemper, the Yazoo, and the
Carrollton tragedies. In all the reign of passion
that has followed the war of races in the South, I
can find no imitation of the exclusion of a Curtis
from a public hall by the Republican Mayor of
Philadelphia. These are unpleasant contrasts to
present, but between the accusers of the North and

the accused of the South there must one day be truth, and I shall not hinder its early coming.

Nashville gives an impressive illustration of the progress of the higher education of the blacks in the South. The Fisk University is one of the conspicuous monuments which dot the many beautiful hills about the city, and the citizens of the capital regard it with pride and cordial sympathy. Among the officers who were stationed at Nashville after the close of the war was General Fisk, out of whose kind heart and thoughtful spirit this great work was projected, and by whose energetic labors it was carried on. The funds raised were not sufficient to complete all that was necessary for the students, and a party of colored men and women, gifted with fine voices and musical genius, visited the different cities, and, indeed, crossed the Atlantic, for the purpose of earning money to build Jubilee Hall, which building was necessary in connection with that already provided. The professors, with their families, and the students live in the large building, while the chapel, classrooms, laboratories, etc., are in Jubilee Hall. There are more than three hundred students being benefited by the thoughtful kindness of those who thus labored in their behalf. The intelligent, earnest countenances presented told how true is the saying, "Education makes the man, the want of it the fellow." The destiny of the future of their race is largely within their labors and the labors of the thousands of colored teachers in the field. The minutes were too few to enjoy fully the lesson of the Fisk University, but the general and earnest interest manifested by the students and the beautiful parting song they gave told that advancement is no longer the exclusive attribute of the whites.

JEFFERSON DAVIS.

A JOURNEY through the South for the study of the currents of opinion and the present condition and probable progress of the reconstructed States, would be incomplete without a visit to the one man who must stand in history as the front of the overthrown Confederacy. A drive of five miles from Mississippi City through the sand and straggling pines which skirt the Gulf bay exhibits the same general dilapidation among the old-time summer homes, which were once the favorite retreats of the *élite* of New Orleans in the sickly season. The shore of the bay has a number of palatial plantation-houses, but they have fallen into the sweeping decay that marks them as relics of an age that has gone. The only one that seems to have been carefully preserved from the desolation that surrounds it is the Dorsey place, now the home of Jefferson Davis. In a forest of green live-oaks, richly-laden orange-trees, and a profusion of vines and flowers, a large frame plantation-house is presented. It is a single story in height, and has the regulation pillars and broad verandas of the aristocratic Southern mansion. There the ex-Confederate President lives with his nephew, General Davis, and their joint families. The ex-Queen of the Confederate Court is a stout, handsome, cultured, and genial woman; and a daughter, a strongly-marked copy of the mother, possesses unusual attractions of both person and intellect. The house is furnished with every regard for comfort, as the well-worn easy-chairs and lounges and the hall and parlor divans faithfully attest, and the walls are decorated with ancient paintings and modern bric-à-brac, while the wide chimney-place and capacious mantel tell how the cheerful pine fire sparkles when a chill or a stray frost silences the song of the mocking-bird and the bloodthirsty serenade of the mosquito. Soon after I had been politely bowed into the parlor, Jefferson Davis entered alone, and his greeting was the cordial welcome of the proverbial hospitality of the South. I confess to disappointment in the general appearance of the man who stands in history to-day as the soldier-statesman without a country. I expected to find the strongly-marked traces of a grievously disappointed life, and severe civility and studied reticence in discussing all things of the past; but those who believe Jefferson Davis to be misanthropic in temperament and embittered against the nation and the world greatly misjudge him. Nor is he the broken invalid that he is generally regarded.

His yet abundant locks and full beard are deeply silvered, and his face and frame are spare as they always have been; but his step is steady, and the hard lines of his brow, which are so conspicuous in his pictures, are at once effaced when he enters into conversation. Instead of impressing the visitor as a political recluse who has no interest in the land to whose citizenship he will live and die a stranger, he at once invites the freedom of the planter's home by chatting without reserve, save when his contemporaries are likely to be criticised, when he adroitly and pleasantly turns the discussion into inoffensive channels. He is yet the same positive man in all his convictions and purposes that made him the leader of a causeless rebellion. He well understands that he cast the die for empire or for failure that must make him alien to the country and the world, and that he lost; and he knows that he is to-day the

most powerless of all men in the land to retrieve the
fortunes of those who followed him to bereavement
and sacrifice. He reads aright the inexorable judgment that makes him execrated for the Confederacy,
while his equally guilty subordinates have been welcomed to the fatted calf. His Vice-President, who
followed the slave empire afar off when doubt and
darkness gathered about it, made haste to scramble
over the ruins of the Confederacy, and regain the seat
in Washington from which he seceded with Davis to
aid in guiding the rebellion. Two of his unnoted
warriors have sat in Republican Cabinets; Lee's
ablest lieutenant was the Republican Minister to
Turkey; the man who marched the first regiment of
volunteers to Charleston, and who served as Confederate Senator until Appomattox became historic, died
as the Republican Minister to Russia; and Senate,
House, and the Washington departments swarmed
with men under Republican rule who were abreast
with Jefferson Davis in every effort to dismember the
Republic; but Davis is the embodiment of humiliation, while his fellows go in and out without dis-
pleasure. I heard no allusion to or complaint of this
injustice, but it is plainly evident that Davis entirely
appreciates it, and that he believes he would not be

consistent with himself and the grave responsibilities he assumed, however mistaken he may have been in assuming them, if he did not deliberately remain an alien to the government that he more conspicuously than all others struggled to overthrow. He could not help the South or himself by seeking or accepting restoration to citizenship, and he is wisely content with stubborn faith in the rectitude of his lost cause.

I have long desired to know the exact truth from the fountain of Southern knowledge on the subject in regard to several important events of the war, and I was agreeably surprised at the freedom with which Mr. Davis met my inquiries. Why Beauregard was ordered to fire upon Anderson in Fort Sumter, after his surrender was inevitable at a specified time without assaulting the flag, has never been entirely understood. It was the act of madness, as it made division in the North impossible, and I have always believed that the real cause of the order to open fire was to unify the South and end the threatening movements for reunion on terms. Mr. Davis answered promptly and emphatically that the order was given solely because faith had been broken by the Lincoln administration in attempting

to reinforce Anderson, and that the South needed
no war to solidify its people. I think he errs in
underestimating the probable power of the movement in the South for concentration before the war,
but it is evident that in deciding to issue the fatal
order for the assault upon Sumter he believed the
Confederacy invincible, and defiantly resented what
he regarded as a violation of the pledge of the Federal government. That act practically consolidated
the North," and thenceforth the Confederacy was a
fearfully hopeless venture. On another important
point he answered with the same freedom. When
asked whether the aggressive movement of Lee that
culminated at Gettysburg was adopted as purely
military strategy or the offspring of political necessity inside the Confederacy, he answered that it was
the wisest of both military and political strategy,
but that it was not dictated at all by political considerations. He said that the wisdom of the military movement was proven by the recall of Meade
from Virginia and the transfer of both armies to
Northern soil; but, he soberly added, the battle was
a misfortune. The chances were equal, as he regarded it, for military success, and that would have
deranged the whole plan of the government and

impaired its resources for the campaign of that year. As a military movement, Mr. Davis says the Gettysburg campaign had the entire approval of Lee, and there were no political divisions in the South to dictate any departure from the wisest military laws. I desired, also, to know whether, at the time of the Hampton Roads conference between Lincoln, Seward, Stephens, and others, Mr. Davis had received any intimation from any creditable source that Mr. Lincoln would assent to the payment of four hundred millions as compensation for slaves, if the South would accept emancipation and return to the Union. He answered that he had no such intimation from any source, but that if such proposition had been made, he could not have entertained it as the Executive of the Confederacy. He said that he was the sworn Executive of a government founded on the rights of the States; that slavery was distinctly declared to be exclusively a State institution, and that such an issue could have been decided only by the independent assent of each State. Some of them, he added, would have accepted such terms at that time, but others would have declined it, and peace was, therefore, impossible on that basis.

Mr. Davis discussed the present attitude and future prospects of the South with manifest interest and great candor. While he is not and cannot be a factor in attaining any desired political results for the South, he shares the hopes expressed by the great mass of the more intelligent Southern people, that all the difficult problems will yet be wisely solved by gradual advancement and final harmony of races and sections. He was unreserved in expressing the belief that a civil service in the South that would insure fidelity to government and people could not fail to end partisan or sectional issues, and unite both North and South in the promotion of the material interests of the whole country. His discussion of the relations of the two sections was thoroughly philosophical and statesmanlike, and while he will remain the one adjudged stranger to the Republic, he hopes yet to see the South prosperous in common with a prosperous North, and the scars of war and the bitterness of sectional dispute healed forever. Next to a Southern Slave Confederacy, he believes a free Union the best government for the Republic.

MRS. JAMES K. POLK.

THERE are many elegant residences on the hills about the beautiful Capitol of Tennessee, but one palatial home within a square of the public grounds cannot fail to attract the special attention of the sojourner. A wide lawn extends back some fifty yards from the street, where stands an old-time Southern mansion, with the colossal pillar that is the pride of the plantation architect, and the wide halls and capacious rooms so common in the best residences of the South. The walls and doors and shades bear unmistakable evidence of age, with here and there the stealthy prints of decay, but the easy-chairs on the portico, the cordial welcome extended by the servant, and the profusion of well-worn sofas and rockers, located with the irregularity that unconventional comfort dictates, tell how freely the gates open to the visitor. This is the home of Mrs. Polk, widow of the ex-President of the United States, who has sur-

239

vived her honored husband nearly four decades, and
has seen all his contemporaries pass away. Although
the storms of more than fourscore years have fallen
upon her she is yet cheerful as a lass of twenty, and
her smile is as natural and as free as it could have
been when it was lavished upon the generation that
is now forgotten. The brown curls of her youth are
yet faultlessly imitated, although threaded in silver,
on her finely-cast forehead, and her turban crown
of black with the widow's silver lining gives her the
appearance of a genial and well-preserved dame of
sixty summers. Her step is feeble, but her eyes are
scarcely dimmed by the long lapse of more than
patriarchal years, and her memory is unabated. She
does not tolerate in a conventional way the many
trespassers upon her time, but she greets all with
queenly dignity, and yet with that generous welcome
that makes every visitor mark his or her visit as one
of the fadeless memories of life. She is glad to have
the stranger as her guest, and she talks of both the
past and the present with a degree of interest, intelligence, and freedom from the common weaknesses of
age which charm every class of listeners. I had
never met either her or her husband, and I feared that
my visit would be an intrusion upon the retirement

of a feeble woman harassed by the calls of the curious, but she met me with the expression, " I saw by
the morning papers that you were in the city, and
I hoped that you would not pass me by." A visit
that was intended to be only the briefest of calls was
thus prolonged into hours, and then reluctantly termi-
nated only because other and imperative engagements
could not be further encroached upon. She is a constant reader of the leading newspapers, and is as well
informed about the events of the present as she was
of the politics and conflicts of the days of Clay,
when her husband triumphed over the most idolized
political leader of our history, and her discussion of
Clay and his galaxy of brilliant contemporaries is
wonderfully interesting and instructive. She realizes
that times and customs have greatly changed, both
in the nation and in its capital, and she speaks of it
with all her natural devotion for the customs of the
past, but with a delicacy and liberality which forbid
offence to the most positive convictions. She is so
universally beloved by all parties and classes in Tennessee, that her little fortune in State bonds—all she
possesses in the wide world—has been, by unbroken
consent, exempted from the flood-tide of repudiation
that has defaulted in the interest due to other credi-

tors. Republican and Democrat, white and black, high tax and low tax,—all agree that the interest shall be paid promptly on the debt held by her, and in all the mutations of public credit in Tennessee there has been no default to the widow of James K. Polk. She spoke freely of the honors she has enjoyed, but her eye brightened with all the lustre of youth when she named the ovations given to her husband when retiring from power, and the kindness shown to her by her own State, and by strangers from every section, as the most cherished of all the distinctions of her life. "The worship of the setting sun," she said, "is not the common homage of the world, and it outweighs all the flattery and pomp of power."

Just forty-one years ago, on the 5th of March, 1845, Mrs. James K. Polk entered the White House at Washington as the wife of the President and chief lady of the land. She had then reached even beyond the full noontide of her years, as more than forty winters had entered into the story of her honored life. Few of the people of the present have personal recollections of the gentle grace and easy dignity with which she shone in the circles of the nation's most cul-

tured men and women of that day; but the pleasant tradition of the White House that makes the
name of Mrs. Madison illustrious as the most
beloved of the early mistresses of the home of
the President, is supplemented by the lingering
memories and oft-repeated tributes in every section
of the land, which tell of the well-merited and
more than generous homage paid to Mrs. Polk
while presiding as the central figure of the social
jewels of the Republic. She welcomed at her hospitable board the Clays, the Websters, the Calhouns,
the Bentons, the Bells, the Buchanans of our history, and in all the bitter conflicts of the disputing
giants of the last generation, the more than respect that grows into the reverence of affection
was commanded from all by the lady of the
White House. Soon after the retirement of her
honored husband from the highest civil trust of
the world he was suddenly called, in the full
vigor of his life, to join the great majority beyond,
and the whole nation mourned the common bereavement it suffered by the death of James K.
Polk. Widowed and alone, Mrs. Polk fitted the
dreamless couch of the dead in the green lawn
that fronted their beautiful home in Nashville, and

there the ashes of her lord repose, in daily view
of the one whose life has had a single sorrow
that makes all other sorrows fade into forgetfulness. Unforgetting as if unforgotten, the modest
panoply that covers the tomb of her buried love
is the shrine to which go out the devotions of
each succeeding day, and the room in the homestead where the ex-President sank calmly into the
sleep of death has stood unaltered and unoccupied,
save as widowed love returns to the altar of
blighted but unwearied affection. Thus while a
full generation has come and gone, Mrs. Polk has
kept faithful vigil over her husband's dust and
her husband's honor; and she has seen eleven
Presidents follow Mr. Polk in the chair he so
worthily filled.

Of all the women of the land, the widow of
James K. Polk has long been accorded the largest
measure of the nation's respect and reverence.
While ever faithful to the one bright memory of
her long and beautiful life, she has made friend
and stranger, old and young, high and low, welcome to her hospitable home, and the visitor to
Nashville who does not cross the threshold of
Mrs. Polk and receive her welcome, is forgetful

of one of the most delightful opportunities. Every day her house hears the greeting of the journeying stranger, and the bright faces of childhood, of early man and womanhood, and of ripened age come and go as the grand old lady smiles upon them with the weight of more than fourscore years upon her. I lately saw her in the midst of a large reception she had given to Philadelphia ladies, and although bowed with age, she was sprightly as any of the many accomplished ladies who assisted in her queenly hospitality, and her unclouded memory and unabated interest in public men and public events, made her ever the centre of attraction for all. She spoke freely and most intelligently and accurately of the political conflicts of her husband's time, of the great men of Tennessee who were his contemporaries, and of the men of national renown during her husband's administration. She spoke of peace and of war, and she gave the most impressive illustration that the whole country could furnish of the beauty of Mr. Lincoln's memorable teaching,—" With malice toward none; with charity for all." Mrs. Fall, her niece, and her accomplished daughter, most gracefully performed the active duties of the hostess, and there was regret visible on every face, alike of neighbor when good-by was said, and of the stranger when farewell was uttered.

THE HOME AND GRAVE OF CLAY.

"HERE's to you, Harry Clay!" is a sentiment that lingers with me in the grateful memories of forty years ago. It was the toast to hearty bumpers from Maine to Texas, and it inspired men of soberest mien as well as of fervid enthusiasm, North and South, East and West. The love for Henry Clay was the grandest devotion the people have ever shown to a great leader. Washington was more reverenced and Jackson more potential, but the affection of the followers of Clay will stand throughout all time, as it has stood in the past, the sublimest monument of the love of the American people for a popular chieftain. Although more than the period of a generation has elapsed since the defeat of Henry Clay, his name yet quickens memories in every section of the Union, and eyes grown lustreless by age sparkle as with the fire of youth at the memory of "Harry of the West." Of all the great popular leaders of the

Republic, he was the most magnetic, the grandest in eloquence, courage, and patriotism, the noblest Roman of them all.   Before he had passed the noontide of his illustrious life he was Senator, Speaker, Commoner, Pacificator, and who of all the nation's jewels in statesmanship approached such distinction?   He was ambitious; but who that loved his country as did Clay, and was the most beloved of all his countrymen, could have been less ambitious than was he? He suffered defeat in grasping for the highest honor of the Republic, and he keenly shared the sorrow of his worshippers when another was crowned with the laurels he had so nobly earned; but the victor, after creditable exercise of the great office, is remembered only as dating and moulding a chapter in the nation's annals, while the vanquished keeps in perpetual greenness the undying love of the people.   More than thirty years have passed since the death of Clay, but his memory is as soft, sweet music on distant waters to the sixty millions of the Union whose honor, prosperity, and greatness he so bravely battled for.

I find myself for the first time in Lexington, the home of Clay.   Grand as it is in the associations which gather about his lustrous name and career, it is not the Lexington that called the "Mill Boy of the Slashes" to seek home and fame in the Kentucky wilderness. When he turned his youthful face toward the setting sun in 1797, and cast his lot in the outpost of civilization, the Lexington of that day was regarded as the future inland commercial centre of the South and West. It was baptized at the campfire of pioneers by the patriotic impulse that welcomed the news of the Lexington battle in Massachusetts, and Virginia culture and refinement came to the land of Boone and made the new Lexington the Athens of the West. Clay and Pope both came from the Old Dominion to rise with the most promising and cultured people of the new Commonwealth, and both honored it in later years in the Senate of the United States. And their dreams of social and commercial pre-eminence for their new Western home long seemed to be certain of fulfilment. Before Clay had reached national distinction as Commoner, Lexington had become the great commercial centre of the West, with Cincinnati, Louisville, and all the near West and South seeking it as a wholesale trading depot. Its Law and Medical colleges rivalled even the great cities of the East, and its temples of learning were the pride of the nation. Transylvania

University was the Yale of the South, with its charter from parent Virginia antedating the independence of the Colonies. The population of Lexington was once thrice that of Louisville or Cincinnati, and it was the centre of Southern intellect, refinement, and elegance. It has furnished the most illustrious line of statesmen of any city or county in the Union. Nine residents of Fayette County have borne the high commission of proud Kentucky to the United States Senate, and among them were such memorable names as Clay, Marshall, Breckenridge, and last, though not least, the present Senator Beck, who cast his first vote for Clay in 1844; and twice that number have made the name of Lexington familiar in the House of Representatives.

But commerce is shifting as the sands of the sea, and the Lexington that Henry Clay dreamed of and saw in commercial and social pre-eminence three-score years ago, is now, as compared with that day, another sweet Auburn, grandest in the fragrant memories of fugitive greatness. The steamboat's hoarse song was heard on the Ohio; commerce fled to worship at new altars, and the city lots which sold at fabulous prices in the suburbs of Lexington have long been gathered back into heartsome and bountiful blue-grass farms. I spent a most interesting and instructive morning here with one of the few surviving contemporaries of Clay when Lexington was the boasted Athens of the West. Benjamin Gratz* has braved the storms of ninety-one winters. He tells of Philadelphia when a city less than the present Louisville, and of Lexington as the boasted inland city of the continent. He once pointed to Transylvania University in its grandest distinction as part of his own work, and he shared every joy and sorrow of Henry Clay. His eyes are sightless, and his fine form bowed by the weight of years, but his face brightens with almost the fervor of youth when he tells the story of the devotion of Lexington to the gallant "Harry of the West." The city of Penn that he left to become part of the future metropolis of the West, now has nearly a million people within its limits, and the Western metropolis, founded so hopefully in the heart of the beautiful and bountiful blue-grass region, is to-day a pretty village, rich in legend and tradition, richer in the nation's records of enduring fame, but with all the glory of early dreams departed.

---

*Now dead.

A drive of a mile southeast along the limestone turnpike that paves the streets of towns and highways about them, brings the visitor to Ashland, the home of Henry Clay. The road is dotted with beautiful suburban residences most of the way on the north, and part of the original Ashland farm is soon presented on the south. It is in beautiful fields, green with the noted blue-grass that is credited with the creation of the famous stock of Kentucky, but it is now the property of the Agricultural College. Farther to the south is the home of John Clay, the only surviving son of the founder of Ashland, who lives the quiet life of a farmer on some two hundred acres of the old homestead. Beyond Ashland is the home of the late Thomas Clay, another son, and it is still in possession of his family; but the Ashland whose aged trees were planted and whose mansion was planned and fashioned by Clay himself, is now the residence of his grand-daughter, Mrs. McDowell, and her accomplished and hospitable husband. It was long the residence of James B. Clay, the only son who reached national distinction as a public man, and who was twice elected to represent the Lexington district in Congress. He died in the prime of life, and the citizens of Lexington and the State contributed to the purchase of the property for an Agricultural College. The College was not successful on the plan adopted, and Colonel McDowell, a Kentuckian of culture and fortune and the husband of the only daughter of Henry Clay, Jr., who fell at Buena Vista, purchased Ashland, and it again became the home of the Clays. The mansion had been rebuilt by James to arrest decay, but the old foundations were untouched, and the new Ashland mansion is the exact counterpart of the original, in both architecture and material, lacking only the sanctity of age. Colonel McDowell welcomes the friends of Clay to the home they regard as one of the shrines of patriotism and statesmanship, and his wife hears with filial pride the homage paid to the grandsire she more than idolizes. She is a thorough Clay, with all the marked features and complexion of her grandfather, softened in refined and elegant womanhood. The architecture of the house is as original and novel as it is beautiful. A pillared portico faces Lexington to the northwest, from which the imposing statue of Clay, two miles distant in the Lexington Cemetery, is visible between the forests which skirt the road and town, and single-storied wings with gables to the front flank the main

structure and add to its palatial proportions and internal comfort. The capacious grounds are a forest
of shade, variegated in type and threaded with walks
and drives and beautiful with shrubs and flowers.
It is a home worthy of Henry Clay, and that ex-
hausts the power of eulogy. Colonel McDowell in-
herited Clay's love for horses, and his stable would
have delighted Clay when he was miscalled the
horse-racer, because he believed that men and
women, and all the creatures committed to their
guardianship, should attain the highest measure of
perfection. The quality of his stable may be understood when I speak of "Dictator," a twenty-year-old
horse, for whom he paid twenty-five thousand dollars
only a few weeks ago, and could sell him at an advance to-day, and of a filly for whom he refused ten
thousand dollars at two years of age, and they were
but two of many kindly exhibited, the least valuable
of which as yearlings would rate in the thousands.
"Dictator" is, I learn, the most noted horse on the
continent, and the royal disdain with which he steps
the earth leaves no doubt of his self-appreciated
nobility. All that is about Ashland has the appearance of grandeur. Its gently undulating fields, neat
as a Lancaster model farm; the clearly exhibited

fertility of the soil; the high-bred cattle grazing on the blue-grass coated lawns, and the primeval forests which freshen the fascinating landscape and stand as sentinels over the bountiful fields, all tell why the home of Henry Clay was to him the dearest spot of earth.

Turning from the hospitable home of the descendants of Clay, it is most natural for the visitor to bend his steps to the grave of the great Commoner. No direction is needed, as it towers above town and forest, and guides the worshipper to the shrine he seeks. On the northwestern suburb of the town is the Lexington Cemetery, one of the most beautiful resting-places for the dead I have ever visited. It is grandly and bountifully shaded by forest-trees, variegated with evergreens, and fragrant with flowers. The ground is broken into abrupt undulations, and the little hillocks and sudden ravines are all dotted with the records of the dreamless sleepers of this lovely City of the Silent. Near the centre, on a gentle eminence with a large velvety lawn around it, are the grave and monument of Henry Clay. A broad base of Kentucky limestone, twenty feet high, encloses the dust of the beloved and lamented statesman, and by his side is the partner of his joys and sorrows, who survived him a full decade. Facing the sunny South is an open grating that offers full view of the beautifully chiselled marble tombs which contain the dust of the Clays. On the top of the marble sarcophagus are the simple words, " Henry Clay," and on the side, in letters so plain that the passer-by can read, is the following memorable public utterance by Clay shortly before his death:

I CAN WITH UNSHAKEN CONFIDENCE APPEAL TO THE DIVINE ARBITER FOR THE TRUTH OF THE DECLARATION THAT I HAVE BEEN INFLU-ENCED BY NO IMPURE PURPOSE, NO PERSONAL MOTIVE, HAVE SOUGHT NO PERSONAL AGGRAN-DIZEMENT; BUT THAT IN ALL MY PUBLIC ACTS I HAVE HAD A SOLE AND SINGLE EYE, AND A WARM DEVOTED HEART, DIRECTED AND DEDI-CATED TO WHAT, IN MY BEST JUDGMENT, I BE-LIEVED TO BE THE TRUE INTERESTS OF MY COUNTRY.

On the large base is erected a round column of white limestone, nearly one hundred feet in height, and on the pinnacle is the life-like statue of Clay, facing the home his name and love have made im-mortal. With all his grandeur of character and attainments, his destiny was dust to dust, the common destiny of all; and the heart and tongue whose eloquence inspired the liberty-loving people of every clime are silenced forever, but his memory and his teachings will endure while the Republic lives. After half a century of distinction in both hemispheres, and victories and defeats which are alike immortal, the story ends in the peaceful shades of Lexington Cemetery, and records, after all, only the brief but fretful journey from the cradle to the grave.

THE END.

www.ingramcontent.com/pod-product-compliance
Lightning Source LLC
Chambersburg PA
CBHW030801020726
47499CB00006B/1718